Ancient British Hill Figures

The Cerne valley with the ribs of the Cerne Giant in the foreground.

Rodney Castleden

S. B. Publications

*To John and Celia Clarke
and for Penelope Lively*

First published in 2000 by S. B. Publications,
c/o 19 Grove Road, Seaford, East Sussex BN25 1TP

ISBN 1 85770 103 8

Designed and typeset by CGB, Lewes
Printed by Adland Print Group Ltd
Unit 11, Bellingham Trading Estate, Franthorne Way,
London SE6 3BX

CONTENTS

ABOUT THE AUTHOR

The results of Rodney Castleden's many researches into landscape processes and prehistory over the last thirty years are published in fourteen books and eighty magazine articles. He has carried out archaeological fieldwork on sites as varied as Bronze Age Knossos, Stone Age Stonehenge and English hill figures of less certain age, including the notorious Cerne Giant, offering ground-breaking new interpretations of each site he studies. He is currently exploring the Dark Age reality behind the legend of King Arthur.

He is a teacher by profession and by instinct, and an intellectual explorer, believing that academics have a duty to communicate with general readers, offering clear, honest and well-informed accounts of their work. He also believes in the importance of retrieving the thought-worlds of past cultures; the past offers keys to the future.

By the same author:

Classic Landforms of the Sussex Coast.
The Wilmington Giant: the Quest for a Lost Myth
The Stonehenge People: an exploration of life in Neolithic Britain, 4700—2000 BC
The Knossos Labyrinth: a New View of the 'Palace of Minos' at Knossos.
Minoans: Life in Bronze Age Crete
Book of British Dates
Neolithic Britain: New Stone Age Sites of England, Scotland and Wales
The Making of Stonehenge
World History: a Chronological Dictionary of Dates
The Cerne Giant
Knossos, Temple of the Goddess
Out in the Cold: Ideas on Glaciation
The English Lake District

ACKNOWLEDGEMENTS

The author would like to thank the following for their help in many different ways in the preparation of this book:

John and Celia Clarke; Gerald Pitman; Lady Gaie Vickers; Gordon Armstrong and Richard Philcox of the Sussex Archaeological Society; David Miles, Director of the Oxford Archaeological Unit; David Thackray and Martin Papworth of the National Trust; and Andrew Woodcock and Martin Brown, East Sussex County Archaeologists.

Front Cover photograph of Uffington White Horse reproduced by permission of English Heritage Photographic Library.

1

The Ancient Figures

From the earliest times, people have made works of art. From the emergence of *Homo sapiens sapiens* 40,000 years ago, people have drawn and painted, large and small, on any convenient surface. From the very beginning there are paintings on the walls and ceilings of caves, carvings on the smooth surfaces of rock outcrops. It was a natural development to graduate from these to making huge drawings covering entire hill sides, and the idea must have occurred independently to communities that were widely separated geographically.

Although there is a tendency to think of hill figures as a uniquely British phenomenon, they have been found in the Rockies, the Atacama Desert, in France (the hammer near Tours), Hungary (an eagle), and North Africa (a white horse). England nevertheless has far more hill figures than any other country. There are seventeen surviving white horses, eleven within Wessex alone, two surviving giants and numerous other images besides. Many have been lost, including at least four more giants.

England offers many opportunities for this art form. There are large areas of chalk downland with long, sinuous escarpments stretching for miles across the countryside and presenting the artists with steeply tilted easels. The chalk soils are thin and the green turf provides a strong dark foil for the giant white scraperboard images scratched through them. The outcrop of Jurassic limestone running across country parallel to the chalk is almost as well suited, so the landscapes of southern and eastern England are ideal for hill figures. However, the location map on page 108 shows that large tracts of potential hill figure country do not have ancient hill figures, and the questions that this raises need to be answered later.

The hill figure is a piece of artwork cut into the turf, usually on a hill slope so that it can be seen and appreciated from the ground. Usually the drawing is very large, so that it can be seen and recognized from a distance. The image may be soil-cut; that is, only the turf is removed so that the effect is made by the contrast between the green of the grass and the soil colour, whatever that may be. It may alternatively be rock-cut, and people often assume when they see a white chalk hill figure from a distance that they are looking at the chalk of the bedrock, stripped bare. In practice, this is not often the case. Even where the soil is thin, as it often is on chalk downland slopes, the chalk below is weakened by frost shattering, and would make a poor surface for the figure. Sometimes the soil is thicker than expected, so that trenching down to solid bedrock would take one deeper than practicable.

The solution to this problem has often been to dig out a shallow trough to the shape required and then fill the cavity with chalk rubble up to the level of the grass. This technique is used today on the Cerne Giant – and was used through the last 3,000 years on the Uffington White Horse. It is likely that this was the standard method for creating – and maintaining – hill figures. Recent examination of the Uffington Horse has shown that there are layers of hillwash between the turf and the bedrock. It may be that the original intention was simply to remove the turf and expose dazzling white chalk rock, but that the effect of the exposed hillwash, creamy in some places and brown in others, was disappointing and unsatisfactory. It must have looked like a zebra or a quagga, animals its creators could not have known about, and thus a nonsensical image. This prompted the early iron age creators of the Horse to cover up the discoloured surface with uniformly white chalk rubble: packed down and exposed to the weather, this quickly resembled solid chalk.

Images can be created in two ways. The first is in lines, and the Cerne Giant and Wilmington Giant are classic examples of this method. The second is in silhouette, of which the Uffington White Horse is the most famous example. The line drawing method has some advantages. It involves removing less turf, it enables the artist to show finer detail if required, and it is easier to maintain. However, it has a serious disadvantage – it cannot be seen so easily from long distances. Much, of course, depends on the thickness of the lines. Line width on the Cerne Giant is currently maintained at 40cm, which looks neat but does not give the figure a very striking appearance when viewed from the opposite side of the valley. In antiquity the line width varied round the figure, and exceeded one metre in places. The Long Man is also currently portrayed with undue refinement. The concrete blocks marking his outline are 25cm wide, whereas the original trench cut in the soil was probably 80cm. These broader and bolder lines would increase the visibility and visual power of both giants two or threefold.

The chalk areas are strongly favoured for the creation of hill figures simply because the soil tends to be fairly thin and the tonal contrast between the greenness of grass and the dazzling whiteness of freshly broken chalk is so striking. Inevitably, more hill figures are found in chalk country than outside it. Some hill figures have nevertheless been cut in other rocks, such as the Red Horse of Tysoe and Gogmagog at Plymouth. Some people have suggested that these darker and duller images may have been brightened up by applying different coloured soils or silts brought in from elsewhere. Paint of course is another possibility, in both modern and ancient times, and it is strange how easy it is to forget that paint existed in antiquity and that the Elgin Marbles, for instance, were once brightly coloured. And what about the condom, executed in creosote, that was illegally added to the Cerne Giant? And the message 'GOODBYE HARRY' painted in weedkiller on the North Downs near Wye College for the retiring principal?

Given the enormous size of the drawings, it is rather surprising that until comparatively recently little notice has been taken of them. Some scholars, such as Joe Bettey, have argued that the absence of literary references to specific hill figures proves that they were not made until quite late. The truth is that some at least of the figures are extremely ancient, yet were simply not considered worth documenting.

Times change, values change, interests change. It was only with John Aubrey in the seventeenth century and William Stukeley in the eighteenth that interest in native British antiquities began in earnest. No one wrote about the great henge monument with its megalithic stone circles at Avebury until John Aubrey did so in the mid-seventeenth century. Scholars obsessed with documentation might argue that Avebury must therefore have been built not long before Aubrey saw it, but we know from radiocarbon tests that it was built in 3000 BC. The same arguments apply to hill figures. The Cerne Giant was first formally documented in 1694, but that

The phallus of the Cerne Abbas Giant, with the author top right and the figure's nose, rebuilt by William Keighley, on the skyline.

does not stop it being middle or late Iron Age in origin. The Uffington White Horse was first formally noted on paper in the twelfth century, and studiously omitted from several ninth and tenth century charters listing the landmarks along Uffington's western boundary, but it is known from OSL dating to have existed as long ago as 700 BC.

When Francis Wise wrote a short essay on hill figures as a class of monument in 1742, he was fully aware that he was the first to do so. He even commented, when writing of the Uffington White Horse, that it was:

'. . . an antiquity of a class that had hitherto escaped the observation of the curious: so far from being taken notice of by our antiquaries, that its existence had in a manner been denied by one of the greatest character among them.'

This was a reference to Camden's rather slighting reference to the Uffington hill figure. It was possible, Camden had said, to imagine the form of a horse on the hillside. Wise was right. No one had taken the trouble to write about this unique class of monument before. Wise showed insight in another way too. He recognised that hill figures were, considered as art, pretty barbarous compared with classical antiquities, but he insisted that they were worthy of attention as they offered information about the people whose art they represented:

> 'But the Monuments, however rude and barbarous, still have their use, and contribute equally to the end proposed.'

The possibilities of this neglected art form are apparently limitless. Or at least were limitless. Planning regulations have effectively put a stop to any further gigantic downland art, at least of a permanent nature, and it has to be said that in the eighteenth and nineteenth centuries, when there were no such restraints, a singular lack of imagination was shown. Why all the horses? Why no Kentish Apple Tree, Suffolk Pig or Norfolk Turkey? Why no Nelson, Wellington or Queen Victoria?

We have a small number of hill figures, or geoglyphs, as some call them, dating from before 1700 and they are extraordinary in appearance. Without doubt significant numbers of ancient hill figures have been allowed to grow over and disappear. There is no way of knowing how many have been lost in this way, but it is possible that with careful research some of them may be recovered.

A great deal of speculation has gone into reconstructing the technique for making hill figures. In reality, as has been proved experimentally, they are quite easy to draw. *The Times* telephoned me in the mid-1990s and asked, with mock concern, whether the Roedean Sixth Formers were out of control. They had, on their final night as schoolgirls, painted a half-size replica of the Cerne Giant on the hockey pitch.

They had obtained a small drawing of the Cerne Giant, marked about ten key points on it, such as shoulders, elbows, knees, measured the distances between them, and scaled them up. Armed with this set of statistics and a couple of tape measures, they marked out the positions of the Giant's key joints on the pitch. Then one girl sketched in the outline with a thin brush, while others viewed the overall composition from a distance to check for errors. This method is known to have been used for several of the modern chalk figures, such as the Cherhill and Alton Barnes Horses and the Wye Crown. One of the Roedean Giant's legs looked wrong, so it was re-drawn. Then the thin line was widened with a broad brush loaded with emulsion paint. The whole outline was completed in about an hour, and at night.

The Times chuckled disbelievingly when, poker-faced and poker-voiced, I explained that this was an exercise in experimental archaeology, but it really did prove that drawing a hill figure is quite easy. The hard work is what follows – digging out the many tons of turf, soil and weathered rock to make an incised outline and filling it with rubble. Harder still, because widely varying social and political conditions come into play, are the long centuries of maintenance and care required to prevent the outline eroding away or grassing over.

The wearisome task of weeding, cleaning and repairing the figure usually has to be carried out at least three times a century to ensure its survival. Frost, rain and the hoofs of cattle, sheep and horses break up the exposed chalk surface, rain washes soil down it, animal dung creates soil directly on it, grass and weeds creep in from the edges and seeds transported by birds and wind spread plants right across it. Chesterton's *Ballad of the White Horse* describes it well;

> The turf crawled and the fungus crept,
> And the little sorrel, while all men slept,
> Unwrought the work of man. . .
> And the grass, like a great green witch's wheel,
> Unwound the toils of men.

There is little doubt in most people's minds when they look at the Cerne Giant or the Long Man of Wilmington that they are looking at images of gods – not necessarily their own gods, nor even gods from a single culture or period. The idea has long been held that these two giants, together with the White Horse of Uffington and a number of other hill figures were badges, totems or talismans adopted by particular ancient British tribes. An additional, rather than alternative, function of hill figures was as signposts, to help travellers find their way in a landscape less differentiated and more heavily wooded than it is today. It seems probable that the Cerne Giant was a billboard, not for Cerne Abbey as has been suggested, but for a tiny wooden temple dedicated to an iron age deity on the hill top.

Others were probably made as seasonal gestures, not intended to endure. The medium of stripped grass packed with rubble was not one for posterity, but more akin to Keats' idea for his own obituary:

> 'Here lies one whose name was writ on water'.

A good modern example of an ephemeral figure is the Grey Man of Ditchling, a cartoon of John Major as the Long Man of Wilmington, wearing a dunce's cap, holding two striped ranging rods and shouting: 'No

More Major Roads'. It was a very specific Friends of the Earth protest against the Conservative government's road building policy, in particular aimed at highlighting the folly of continuing with the Folkestone-Honiton highway project. The figure was painted on the Downs so that it would be seen by large numbers of people during the Tour de France in August 1994. Since that event both the figure and the political cause have evaporated.

Some ancient hill figures were doubtless similarly made for an occasion and abandoned, quickly grassing over and disappearing from memory, but others caught the communal imagination and were carefully maintained over long periods. That some have survived is a tribute to social continuity, and this appeals to a new feeling that history has not after all been dominated by the reigns of kings and queens, wars and the arrival of small numbers of invaders. The evolution of the late twentieth century approach to social history has contributed to a strengthened recognition of the role of hill figures, among many other 'folk institutions', in popular culture. The revival in interest in hill figures is part of the zeitgeist. Through them we can see how ordinary people have maintained loyalty to their local traditions, customs and landmarks, and weeded and patched their hill figures across all manner of social, religious and political boundaries. Another relevant strand is the quest for alternative belief systems. For many the desire for a better world once found expression in formal religion, mainly Christianity in this country, but disenchantment with Christianity began in the nineteenth century and accelerated in the twentieth. Nineteenth century humanists hoped that science would replace religion, but whereas religion had proved too restricting behaviourally, science developed to a point where it was, for most people, far too demanding intellectually.

People have been left with neither the certainties and assurances of formal religion nor the mental structures of true science. Small wonder, then, that in the twentieth century there has been an explosion in fake science (such as proofs that terrestrial civilizations were set up by visiting aliens) fake religion, including watered-down imported religions from other continents; reconstructed ancient pagan indigenous religions; and what can only be called New Age mind-sets, in which personal assertion and revelation take priority over the research findings of academics in many branches of both sciences and humanities. Enigmatic, often of uncertain origin and purpose, at least partly unexplained, apparently defying classification – the older hill figures have inevitably become a focus for those seeking some Alternative Way. As the generations have passed, values and beliefs have shifted, and new meanings have been given to the old images. Local folk-lore is entertaining and always worth hearing, but not a reliable route to the remote past.

Not all hill figures are ancient; in fact the majority of them were made after 1750. The 1933 Whipsnade Lion is one of the most recent, while the Woolbury Horse of 1729 seems to be the oldest in the modern series. This list of the post-1700 figures will serve to clarify which are not ancient:

?1729 Woolbury Horse, Hampshire
?1764 Watlington White Mark, possibly by Edward Horne
1770 Mormond Horse, Aberdeen
1780 Cherhill Horse, Wiltshire by Dr Christopher Alsop
1785 Pewsey Old Horse by Robert Pile
1790 Osmington Horse, an equestrian portrait of George III
?1800 Rockley Horse
1804 Marlborough Horse, Wiltshire, designed by William Canning as a boy and
  made by other pupils at Mr Gresley's school
1812 Alton Barnes, Wiltshire by Robert Pile
1835 Broad Hinton Horse, Wiltshire by Henry Eatwell
1838 Litlington Horse I, East Sussex by the Pagden brothers
1845 Devizes Horse by local shoemakers
1857 Kilburn White Horse, Yorkshire ordered by Thomas Taylor
1864 Broad Town Horse by William Simmonds
1868 Inkpen Horse by Mr Wright
1870 Mormond Stag, Aberdeen by Mr Gardner
1902 Wye Crown, Kent designed by T J Young
1909 Dover Aeroplane, Kent
1916–18 Fovant Badges, Wiltshire depict a map of Australia, a triangle and the
  initials YMCA, and the badges of a number of army regiments including the 6th
  City of London Rifles, Post Office Rifles, London Rifle Brigade, Royal
  Warwickshire Regiment, Devonshire Regiment, Royal Wiltshire Regiment, 7th City
  of London Battalion, Royal Wiltshire Yeomanry, Royal Corps of Signals, and the
  Australian Imperial Air Force
1918 Bulford Kiwi designed by Percy Blenkarne
1922 The Buffs Dragon Badge, Kent by Oliver Mason
1925 Litlington Horse II, East Sussex, a new figure
1933 Whipsnade Lion designed by R. Brook-Greave
1969 Laverstock Panda

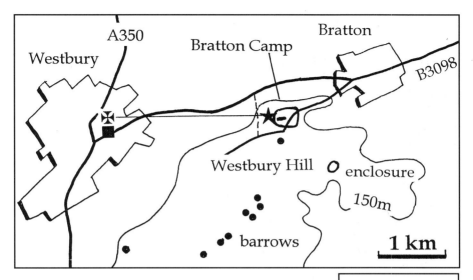

2

Westbury Old Horse

The 1778 horse, about which there is no mystery, replaced and destroyed an earlier horse, about which there is plenty. The 1778 horse is the earliest and most interesting of the Wiltshire chalk horses.

It is the whitest of all the hill figures, its body a large expanse of brilliant white chalk, but it is a very static animal, lacking energy and expression. The horse is 55m long and 33m high and is cut on what must surely be one of the finest sites anywhere for a chalk figure. It is on a steep slope and can be seen from a great distance – as far away as the Mendips in the southwest.

Richard Gough surveyed the Westbury Horse for

LOCATION.

On Bratton Down in Wiltshire, overlooking the Vale of Pewsey, one mile south-west of Bratton. It is on a west facing slope just below the Iron Age hillfort of Bratton Camp.
Park by the roadside on the B3098 halfway between Bratton and Westbury and follow the footpath southwards up the slope. It passes directly below the Horse.
Alternatively, turn off the B3098 in Bratton village and take the minor road westwards through Bratton Camp and walk down to the Horse.

his edition of Camden's *Britannia* just six years before it was replaced by a new version. Of it he wrote:

> 'On the south-west of the hill is a most curious monument unnoticed by Bishop Gibson: a white horse in a walking attitude cut out of the chalk, and to the tip of his ear near one hundred feet high, and from ear to tail one hundred feet long: an undoubted memorial of this important victory [the Battle of Ethandun, AD 848, which Gough took to have taken place at nearby Edington], and like that by which Alfred commemorated his first great victory in Berkshire eight years before'.

Plenderleath called this connection with Alfred's battle a 'local tradition', but there is no evidence that the tradition goes any further back than Wise and Gough. Local people may well have repeated the Wise idea, which has no known ancestry.

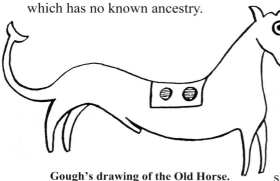

Gough's drawing of the Old Horse.

Gough drew the Old Horse. It is a peculiar looking creature, long and low like a dachshund, with a saddle marked with two discs and a long curving tail ending in a crescent shape. It has one large round eye. The long, sinuous shape suggests the Uffington Horse, and Gough clearly thought of the two horses as a pair, both made by Alfred. Yet his drawing shows a poor looking beast, and we must wonder whether this is really what it looked like. Oddly, Gough himself made no comment on its extraordinary shape, only commenting on it as 'a white horse in a walking attitude cut out of the chalk.' The blandness of the account and the mismatch of the drawing suggest that someone else was responsible for the bizarre drawing. How, in reality, were the circles or discs on the saddle executed in the turf, or the eye for that matter? These details would only have been possible if the image was a line drawing, which it well may have been.

The Reverend W C Plenderleath, in his *White Horses of the West of England*, regretted the obliteration of the older horse, 'ruined by the same unenlightened spirit which has destroyed so many precious historical remains'. It was Mr Gee, Lord Abingdon's aptly named steward, who destroyed the Old Horse and created the new one. Gee's horse is a competent likeness of a real horse, but it somehow lacks the strangeness and mystery of Gough's four-legged cyclops. The new horse has nevertheless changed slightly since it was made and now looks more like a pony. Even so, Plenderleath's drawing of it is very close to how it appears today.

The Westbury Horse as it is today.

One peculiarity of the modern horse is that it faces north, whereas the earlier one faced south. Why did Gee turn it round? In 1885 Plenderleath suggested sensibly that he did not but that Gough's engraver had inadvertently reversed the printed image. His sketch shows how, if both faced north, Gee's remodelling did not involve very much change after all. On the other hand, Plenderleath's drawing exaggerates the size of the Old Horse and it would have been quite possible for the whole of it to fit inside the belly of the New Horse's belly, and Morris

Plenderleath's Old and New horses superimposed.

Marples suggests that this is how the Old Horse disappeared. No trace of it survived because it has been consumed by the new one. Probably both suggestions are right. Gee is unlikely to have turned the horse round, so Gough's engraver was probably responsible for reversing the image of the Old Horse. Marples is probably right in assuming that the Old Horse was destroyed when the much larger body of the New Horse was dug out.

Tom Lethbridge, of course, thought he could still see the Old Horse in the grass in aerial photographs, and drew his own version of the

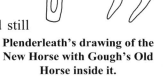

Plenderleath's drawing of the New Horse with Gough's Old Horse inside it.

beast with tusks. But, as he himself admitted, it is possible to persuade yourself of almost anything if you stare long enough at aerial photographs.

The Old Westbury Horse appears on a 1773 map drawn by Andrews and Drury and is clearly shown facing north, incidentally supporting Plenderleath's idea that Gough's drawing was reversed by his engraver. Their horse has well defined hoofs, unlike Gough's, and looks slightly more realistic. But only slightly. It does, it must be admitted, have a distinctly ungainly, camel-like look with its long neck and small head. It is similar to Gough's in having a long, curving, sagging back and belly, so it seems reasonable to suppose that these were real features of the old horse.

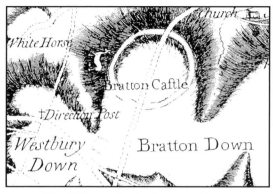

The 1773 map by Andrews and Drury.

The eccentricities of Gough's horse are hard to accept. Did it really have a cyclopean eye, or did Gough's engraver simply misplace it? Why were there no rebuttals of Gough's work in the 1770s and 1780s, when memory of the Old Horse's shape must have been clear? Can the elongation of the body and the relative smallness of the hindquarters be explained by Gough's having sat at the top of the slope near the head, from which place natural foreshortening would correct these distortions? This is in fact quite likely, as the measurements he gives are consistent with a horse of normal proportions, The fish tail is nevertheless hard to explain. Plenderleath came up with the idea that it was a reference to Ceridwen, a Welsh fertility goddess who sometimes shape-shifted into a mare. Taliesin referred to one of Ceridwen's sons as 'strong horse of the crescent'. This sounds fanciful, but it may be that the iconography is part of a Celtic belief system and that the Old Horse was made in the sixth century or earlier.

It is not at all clear when the Old Horse was created. There is little to go on. Although it is obviously earlier than the New Horse, all that is known for certain is that it was made before 1778. Francis Wise suspected that the

Old Horse was relatively recent in origin. In spite of his enthusiasm for an Alfredian white horse at Uffington, he did not think of the Westbury figure as even potentially Saxon. On visiting the site he was told, apparently by local people, that it had been 'wrought within the memory of persons now living or but lately dead.' Wise accepted this view, qualifying his agreement slightly by adding that further inquiry might be desirable.

It may well be that, in spite of Gough's extraordinary drawing, the Old Horse belonged to the eighteenth century just as much as the New Horse. An argument used in favour of a late origin for Westbury is that Camden, Aubrey and Baskerville wrote about Uffington but did not mention Westbury. But this line of argument is a weak one. As in the case of the Cerne Giant, it was quite common for these and other distinguished writers to notice one monument but not another. As Morris Marples points out, argument from silence is notoriously unreliable.

Gough, writing thirty years after Wise, said that he made 'special inquiries' as to the origins of the Westbury Horse, and learned nothing that suggested a recent date. But thirty years is a long time in some villages. Thirty years after the destruction of the Red Horse of Tysoe, no-one in Tysoe knew anything at all about it. Conversely, it may be that the late seventeenth century cutting of the Westbury Horse that Wise seems to have heard about was actually a major scouring or even a recutting on the 1778 scale. There could conceivably have been a horse there before. In favour of the antiquity of the old horse is the open-endedness of the legs of Gough's drawing. This implies that he was unable to trace the legs any further as they petered out down the slope.

This is significant, because it is exactly what happened to the Long Man of Wilmington. Although that figure seems to have been grass-covered throughout the eighteenth and most of the nineteenth centuries, the feet were identifiable in 1710, although not by 1850. Drawings done at the later date clearly show the lower legs fading and the feet disappearing, which explains how the mistake was made in 1874 in the restoration of the feet. The implication is that if the horse's feet were entirely untraceable in 1772 they were cut more than 100 years earlier.

This is circumstantial arguing, it has to be admitted, as we cannot know how much or how little trouble Gough went to in trying to ascertain these details. Too much should not be made to rest on the detailed form of

Gough's drawing. If the body of the horse was an area of exposed chalk, as Gough's account implies, how was the 'line drawing' of the saddle with its two spots achieved? Was the saddle an area of preserved turf, while the spots and the horse's back were cut chalk? And how was the eye drawn? Either the horse on the hillside was a simple line drawing, like the engraving itself, or it was as Gough's phrase 'white horse' strongly implies solid white, like the modern horse, and the details were made up by Gough or his engraver.

All that can be said, in the end, is that the Old Westbury Horse, according to Gough at least, was long and curving, and primitive in style too, so it was similar to the Uffington White Horse. On the other hand, Wise, writing in the mid-eighteenth century, thought it was made in the seventeenth century, so it may have been a pseudo-primitive drawing – in fact, a fake.

3

Watlington White Mark

A tall thin triangle, 59.4m (195ft) high and with a base 7.8m (25ft 6ins) wide, has been cut through the turf and thin soil to the chalk bedrock in a rectangular clearing in the hawthorn woodland. Below the tall isosceles triangle, pictured right, is a rectangle 9.5m wide and 5m deep, separated from the triangle by a grass strip 2.5m wide, and clearly part of the hill figure design. Overall, the figure is 67m on a base 9.5m wide. This is one of the simplest, most graceful and yet most puzzling of all hill figures. Its geometric, abstract shape makes it a real enigma.

The Mark is like a long tapering spear point – an

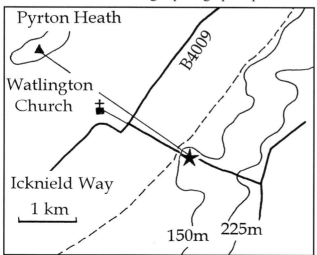

30m

20m

10m

LOCATION.

On the face of the Chiltern scarp south-east of Watlington. From the B4009, turn at the north east edge of the village into Hill Road, which runs right up the escarpment. Park at the foot where the pavement ends and take the unmarked path on the right after the last house, No. 92. After a few metres take the right-hand path to the foot of the figure. To explore Christmas Common, the wooded hilltop above the figure, go on up the road to the National Trust car park on the right.

Pyrton Heath

B4009

Watlington Church

Icknield Way

1 km

150m 225m

The Watlington Mark, showing part of the rectangular base.

arrow pointing south-south-east. Is there, perhaps, some significance in the direction it is indicating? Paul Newman suggests a connection with the equinoctial rising sun, but this is not convincing. For one thing there is no prehistoric site in the Watlington area presenting itself as a likely viewpoint for the sunrise. An association with prehistoric features, either below or above, would lend support to a prehistoric origin for the Mark, but nothing is visible. It is unfortunate that Watlington Hill is covered by a dense hawthorn woodland, which makes it hard to see whether any barrows or other ancient earthworks exist there. The literature, admittedly not always a certain indicator, suggests that nothing of this nature has been observed.

If the Mark is not prehistoric it may be a late arrival. It has been said that it was made in 1764 either by a local landowner, Edward Horne, or by the vicar of Watlington. The obelisk was a favourite architectural feature in landscape gardening in the eighteenth century so it would be understandable if a landowner created a two-dimensional representation of an obelisk to improve the view from his house.

The local tradition is that the villagers wanted a spire for the church but there were insuffcent funds, so the Mark was created as a substitute, resolving the problem with minimum cost. This sounds like a piece of fakelore or nineteenth century post-rationalisation, but it must be said that the shape and size of the mark are about right for a church spire, and the rectangular block underneath could well represent the church tower. In further support is the fact that the church is directly in front of the mark and in line with it. The church still has no spire, apart from this spectre among the thyme, orchids, dogwood and self-heal. Unfortunately, the 1764 church spire story, first documented in 1851, has not been corroborated from any eighteenth century source. It may or may not be true.

The Mark's proximity to the Bledlow and Whiteleaf Crosses suggests that looking at the three chalk marks together might provide the answer, but that answer has not so far been discovered. One theory is that it is an ancient phallic symbol. There is no particular reason for believing that it is for phalli are not usually pointed. It may belong to the pre-Christian period, but if it does there is no corroborative archaeological evidence from the locality.

Watlington church.

The Watlington Mark is owned by the National Trust, and the warden carefully maintains it by hoeing and brushing away invading plants. Rain washes down the slope eroding the upper areas of the triangle and rectangle and the lower areas are built up with accumulations of chalk silt. As a result, the rectangle is tilting towards the horizontal in much the same way as the body of the Uffington White Horse.

21

4

Whiteleaf Cross

LOCATION

On the Chiltern escarpment facing north west and dominating the Vale of Aylesbury.
In Monks Risborough, turn south east into Peters Lane, then left into Upper Icknield Way. Park and walk up the bridleway between Thorns Close and Greensleeves.
Go up the hill, under the trees, keeping to the right of the electricity sub-station, and through a wooden gate onto the hilltop.
The path leads directly across the base of a mill built on the remains of a bowl barrow.
It is then about 100 metres to the top of the hill figure, which is at the summit of the slope to the right.
Do not attempt to climb up directly to the foot of the globe from further along Peters Lane as it is treacherously steep, and you will accelerate the erosion.

The upper part of this hill figure is a Greek cross 7m (23ft) across. It surmounts a huge triangular base of completely bare chalk which has weathered rather unevenly and is known locally known as 'the globe'. Overall the Cross, which is hemmed in on both sides by beech woods, is 75 metres high and the base is 122 metres wide, but it would appear from the measurements given in earlier accounts that it has changed in shape over time.

Wise gave the base as 57.6 metres wide and the

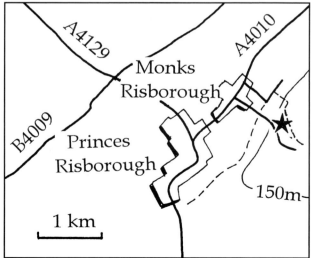

22

overall height as approximately 61 metres which suggests that the base has become significantly broader over the course of two centuries.

Measurements taken in 1848 are consistent with this apparent broadening process. Is what is visible today anything like the original composition, regardless as to whether it was made in seventeenth or the seventh century? It is not possible to read anything into the units of measurement used in the design.

The escarpment is steep, and slopes on the figure vary from 25 degrees at the top to 45 degrees at the bottom. Variable measurements are given, suggesting either changes through time or inaccurate surveys. It is impressive, in spite of its blandness and crudity, and the view from it is no less impressive for it offers a spectacular vista across the Vale. The large expanse of white makes the Cross itself visible from Headington Hill, near Oxford, which is fifteen miles away, and Wise claims he saw it from the White Horse Hill at Uffington, some thirty miles away, although it would certainly not be visible from anything like this distance in its present neglected, greying and overgrown condition.

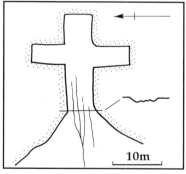

Whiteleaf Cross, with section through gullying.

No one knows when the Cross was made or who made it. A Saxon charter of 903 AD describes the hill as 'the eastern hill crowned with brushwood' and refers to a boundary mark called Wayland's Stock, apparently a venerated post approached by a paved road, but makes no direct mention of the Cross. However, Saxon charters are not reliable sources of information about antiquities of this type.

In 1815 the historian T Warton wrote that it was of great age and that it recalled 'a savage idea of sepulchral pomp'. The Reverend A Baker, writing about it in 1855, saw it as an explicitly Christian monument – 'an awful and almost spectral apparition of the Sign of the Son of Man.'

The Cross seems to declare itself to be a work not only of the Christian era but of committed Christians, a work of devotion, and the existence of a village named Monks Risborough directly below it suggests that a medieval community may have been responsible for making it. The massive triangular

Whiteleaf Cross and, below, the severely eroded and neglected Globe.

Id. Pag. 102.   *Id. Pag. 112.*   *Id. Pag. 123.*   *Id. Pag. 136.*

Comparison with Roman coins suggests a Romano-British origin.

base suggests a representation of a Calvary and it is worth remembering that small artificial hills with crosses on top called calvaries were made in three dimensions in some French villages in the Middle Ages. Smaller versions consisted of wooden crosses on stepped wooden platforms. It has been suggested that the globe was also once stepped, in which case it would make the image as a whole look remarkably like the cross images on some Roman coins. However, it must be borne in mind that the base has widened a great deal during the last 200 years and it may be that in the seventeenth century the base was no more than a slightly flared shaft. The taper given to the shaft would create the illusion, when viewed from the foot of the hill, that the Cross was much taller than it really was.

Another possibility is that Wise's narrowing of the base was an exaggeration, that the base was always a substantial feature, and that it existed before the cross. Marples suggests, as a possibility only, that the base began as a natural, rain-scoured scar. As such it could have been shaped relatively easily into a triangular base for a cross. Whiteleaf appears as Whitcliffe on a 1766 map, which Marples takes as support for a natural chalk scar, but an artificially cut geometric shape might equally have given rise to the name. In 1896 E J Payne suggested that the lower part of the chalk scar was due to the gradual erosion of the road running along the scarp foot. The track

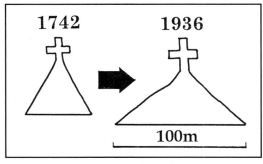

Two versions of the Cross.

from Monks Risborough to the downs crossed the Icknield Way, and he argues that it may have been an important enough junction to justify the erection of a handcross, a wooden fingerpost, at the crossroads. The chalk mark was in its turn a waymark for this crossroads. But all this presupposes that the road junction was an important one, and there seems little reason to see it as such.

There are still other possibilities. If the cross was there first, erosion by rainwash and the feet of visitors – there has been a significant amount of human erosion at Whiteleaf Cross – will have extended the bottom of the shaft progressively downwards. The base may therefore have 'grown' out of the cross. Then again, Wise's elegant tapering base may represent the older part of the image, and it may have started out as a relatively tall and narrow triangle, like Watlington White Mark. As such it may be seen as a two-dimensional equivalent of the obelisk, a favourite eighteenth century ornament. This interpretation would support an origin between 1700 and 1740.

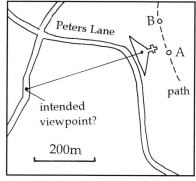

Intended viewpoint according to John North. A is the Neolithic long barrow, B is the bowl barrow.

John North's approach is to ignore any Christian symbolism and focus on relationships with other monuments and, curiously, path and road junctions, inferring from these specific viewpoints from which astronomical events such as starrises could be watched. This revival of a Sixties approach to prehistoric monuments seems a retrograde step, particularly since there is no reason to suppose that the locations of kinks and junctions in paths are in any way significant. It seems unlikely that this approach is going to prove a productive or useful one. In the end, the fact that it is a cross has to be recognised – it is in essence a Christian symbol. There were religious communities not far away during the Middle Ages, and it could be the monks of Missenden Abbey, 8km away, who made the Cross, or the monks at Monks Risborough, just 2km away.

There are dangers, though, with this surmise. The proximity of the Benedictine Priory at Wilmington to the Long Man has been used to

26

explain the creation of that figure, but it is entirely unsatisfactory to propose that the Long Man was the work of 'idle monks'. The proximity of Cerne Abbey to the Cerne Giant has been used to support and reinforce this interpretation, yet it is really most unlikely that a Christian community, however liberal, would have produced an obscene drawing like the Cerne Giant. The proximity of three hill figures to religious houses at the foot of the hill is an intriguing topographical fact, but the 'idle monks' explanation is a deeply unsatisfying one. It does not meet the case. However, there may be a connection of a different kind – perhaps the neutralisation of a pagan focus by the addition of Christian elements.

The idea of Christianising a much older pagan focus is supported by the Whiteleaf Cross's position in relation to two ancient barrows. On the level hilltop immediately above the Cross is a neolithic oval barrow, pleasantly conserved within a wattle enclosure. Not far along the escarpment to the north is the site of a bowl barrow probably dating from the early Bronze Age; not far to the south is a cross-ridge barrier, often used to mark off a section of a ridge as a ceremonial precinct in the Bronze and Iron Ages. There are points in common here with Windover Hill, where two neolithic barrows, a fine bowl barrow and a collection of other round barrows cluster on the ridge above the Long Man. Whether the hill figure was put there as part of the early religious focus, and was therefore pagan and prehistoric, or put there as an antidote, and was therefore Christian and late, is a matter for continuing debate.

In 1742 Wise wrote of the scouring:

'Though the cross is in no more danger of being obliterated than the [Uffington] Horse, yet the like custom prevails of Scouring it up with a Festival; but this has of late years observed no regular revolution. The common people still preserve some imperfect traditions concerning contributions raised upon this occasion, and even from some of the Colleges in Oxford. But if any estates have been formerly charged with the expence, time has long since made void the obligation, and the Scouring is performed at the expence of the neighbourhood, but never without a merry-making'.

In 1855 Baker said that the participation of some of the Oxford colleges still continued, mentioning Christ Church and St John's in particular. Eton College, which held the Manor of Bledlow from 1441, was apparently also still under an obligation to contribute to the maintenance of the Cross.

But there is no documentary evidence to support Baker's assertions.

It may be that he was confusing Christ Church, Oxford with Christ Church, Canterbury. Certainly the Bishop of Dorchester gave the manor to Canterbury in about 993AD.

Traditionally, the owners of the Hamden estate have been responsible for the Cross's upkeep, and in 1826, in accordance with an Act of Parliament, it was repaired the Earl of Buckingham. The Earl's heirs have remained legally responsible for the Cross's maintenance down to the present time. In 1972 the scouring, supervised by the estate's head forester, Mr Watt, took three men eight hours to complete.

As I write, the cross is badly in need of repair; the chalk is discoloured, with vegetation creeping in from the woodland at the sides and some deep gullies scored down the centre of the globe. The lower edge of the globe is crumbling away onto the lane below.

5

Bledlow Cross

The figure, a Greek cross of very simple design, is in a small woodland clearing, with forest pressing in on all sides, so it does not make a huge impact on the landscape. From the B4009 only the upper limb of the cross, which is about 22m (72ft) wide and with arms 4m (13ft) deep, can be seen. The rest of it is obscured by the trees.

The Bledlow Cross lacks Whiteleaf's huge triangular base. Comparisons with its more dramatic neighbour are inevitable, and it seems likely that it was copied from Whiteleaf and therefore must be more recent. It is always a problem arguing from silence, but the two crosses are close together and it

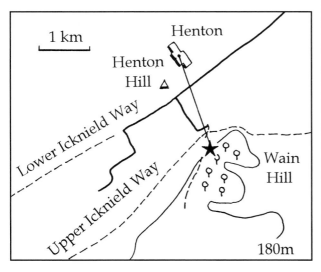

LOCATION

High up on Wain Hill on the Chiltern escarpment. Between Chinnor and Princes Risborough follow the lane from the B4009 signed 'Wainhill only', and if possible park where the tarmac ends. Walk up the unmade road to the scarp foot, where there is a cross-road. Go straight up the tarmac road for a short distance then take the bridleway to the right. This slants along and goes gradually up the slope, passing the hill figure in a small forest clearing in The Cop. Take care – it is hard to find.

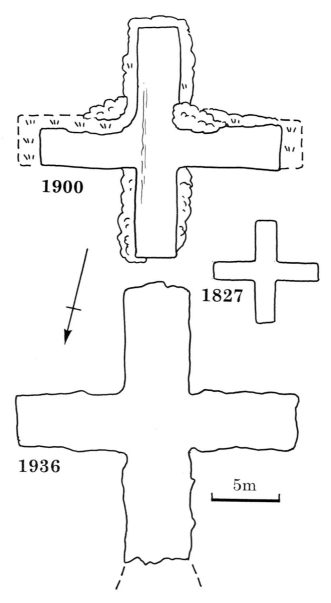

1900

1827

1936

5m

Three plans of the Bledlow Cross.

30

must be significant that Francis Wise, when writing about Whiteleaf Cross, mentions a battle fought at Bledlow but does not mention Bledlow Cross. One of his correspondents, Mr J Collins, wrote to William Stukeley in 1757 about 'a Danish camp at Bledlow, near Princes Risborow; and about two miles east of that place, on the side of a chalky hill, called White Leaf, a large white cross cut in the side of the hill', but he does not refer to the Bledlow Cross. Taken at face value, these silences argue for a late eighteenth century origin for the figure. Marples, however, goes too far when he says they 'prove quite conclusively that the Bledlow Cross is later than 1757.'

The first known documented reference to it is in the *Gentleman's Magazine* of 1827, which states:

> 'On the Bledlow Hills is to be traced the figure of a cross cut in the chalk, but from its having been neglected many years, is now nearly obliterated by the grass and weeds growing on it. A gentleman, who visited it a few days ago, and who is some-what of an antiquary, had the curiosity to measure its dimensions, and to examine it very narrowly. He supposes it to have been made by the Saxons about the time the Whiteleaf Cross (from which it is not very distant) was formed; the mode of working seems to have been by digging squares of six feet, of which there are five, both in the perpendicular and the transverse lines, making a cross of 30 feet long in both lines, and of the width of six feet.'

It is difficult to establish from these reports whether the cross is ancient or not. If the cross was made late, as Wise's and Collins' silence suggests, it should have looked fresher in 1827 than it evidently did. In 1827 it was 'nearly obliterated by the grass and weeds growing on it,' so it must have been neglected for several decades, and could not have been cut or cleaned after 1800. That nevertheless still leaves open the possibility that the cross was cut between 1760 and 1790. Another point emerges from the 1827 description. The Cross seems to have been a lot smaller then than it is now, in fact less than half its present size.

A document dated September 1350 gives a list of felons, including a man named Henry atte Crouche of Bledelowe, which could mean either 'Henry at Bledlow Cross' or 'Henry Attcross of Bledlow'. Either way, there is an association of the word 'cross' with the place 'Bledlow', suggesting an origin earlier than 1350.

In 1885 Bledlow Cross was still in a sorry state. The Reverend A Baker believed it was made by monks and refers to a tradition, presumably local, that the two crosses were the same age. Baker nevertheless thought that Bledlow, the more modest image, was the precursor of Whiteleaf, which he considered to be a more ambitious and later work. He also suggested, less convincingly, that monks had created them as wayside crosses. This seems unlikely, as they were far more difficult for the monks to make than small wooden shrines, as well as significantly less accessible from the road.

A fragment of folklore may or may not tell something of the cross's history. Anyone running across the cross and up and down it, barefoot, will gain fresh energy to complete a walk. This is not datable, and may well be a late accretion, the sort of fakelore that might have been added at any time during the nineteenth century. It really does nothing to help date the figure.

The origins of the Bledlow Cross are obscure, but it was probably intended as a Christian symbol, although the cross was used in pre-Christian times. A Greek cross of marble, made by the Minoans some 1,500 years before Christ, was discovered in the temple at Knossos.

It seems possible that, supposing the Whiteleaf Cross originated as obelisk, with the cross added later to Christianise it, the Bledlow Cross was then made to emphasise that this was a Christian neighbourhood now, whatever it may have been before. The area is spattered with antiquities. There are Neolithic long barrows, Bronze Age round barrows, Iron Age and Romano-British settlements. The ploughed fields at Bledlow have yielded numerous flint scrapers, showing that people lived there 5,000 years ago. It is an area long used, and long visited, but it would be much harder to prove that this hill, or Whiteleaf Hill for that matter, was a pre-Christian religious focus point. Either or both of them may have been.

It is always useful to ask where a hill figure was intended to be seen from. On the map it looks as if the Bledlow Cross faces northwest along Wainhill Lane and that the viewpoint may have been on the top of Henton Hill. But an observer standing on Henton Hill sees the Cross angled to the left, so it is more likely that the intended viewpoint was Henton village or even Skittle Green. Then a significant new fact emerges. From Henton, before the growth of the luxuriant forest cover on the escarpment, there would have been an excellent head-on view of both crosses – Bledlow and Whiteleaf. The likeliest scenario is that someone living at Henton, perhaps the principal landowner in the Middle Ages, looked enviously over at the Whiteleaf Cross in the neighbouring parish and decided to create his own version, near at hand on the stretch of escarpment immediately to the south. Because it was nearer, it was possible to make it smaller yet still very conspicuous. An older origin, however, cannot be ruled out, and the forest on the escarpment points to a much older origin. The woodland is dense, and it would be difficult to clear a patch of it, grub out the tree roots, establish a grass cover and then cut the cross. It is more likely that the cross was there before the trees. The Chiltern scarp was open pasture in the early medieval period, and not planted up with trees until around 1400. The presence of mature yews in the surviving woodland suggests that if the Cross was made in modern times, it could not really have been later than 1400.

Both the addition of the cross to the obelisk at Whiteleaf and the creation of the cross on its own at Bledlow could have occurred in the Middle Ages, before 1350. Wise's omission of the Bledlow Cross does not necessarily indicate a later origin for the figure for he did not, when writing in 1740, mention the Long Man of Wilmington, then known to have been in existence for at least thirty years.

Hill figures were beginning to create a stir of interest after the mid-eighteenth century, with magazine articles and other documentary records beginning to mention them. It would therefore be rather odd for a new figure to have been cut after 1757 without there being any published notice of its creation. The circumstantial evidence points to the Cross being older, with the 1350 reference to 'Henry at Bledlow Cross' and the vegetation history supporting a medieval or earlier origin.

The idea that Bledlow Cross started off as a phallic symbol and was afterwards neutralised or neutered by having arms added to turn it into a cross seems less likely than the other suggestions that have so far come forward, but there are no certainties here. There is a local tradition that the Cross was regularly cleaned at one time, although it has a history of neglect in the twentieth century, with parts of the figure overgrown with grass and shrubs, in spite of the Royal Commission for Historic Monuments' 1912 description of its condition as 'fairly good'.

LOCATION

High on the South Downs halfway between Plumpton village, 4 miles north west of Lewes, and where the bostal joins the South Downs Way. The easiest way to reach it is from the small car park on Ditchling Beacon. Walk east along the Way for about a mile and where the bostal forks left down the escarpment, climb over the farm gate and follow the lower edge of the improved pasture towards the trees. Then take the sheep path along the lower edge of the clump of trees, and this will bring you straight on to the western arm of the Cross.
It can also be reached by walking along the bridleway that goes diagonally upwards, just beneath the Cross, from Plumpton village. For this route, take the south turn at Plumpton crossroads and simply follow the road up to the Cross.

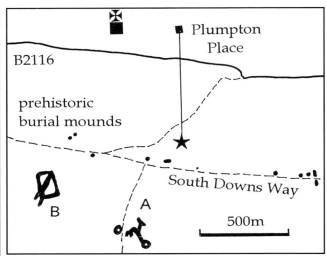

A is the Plumpton Plain Bronze Age settlement, B the prehistoric enclosure

6

Plumpton Cross

This cross is now completely covered with grass and has been for a long time. It stands 180m (585ft) above sea level and, when freshly cut on this 25° slope, would have been visible from a large area of the Vale of Sussex. A substantial trench 0.7 metres deep marks the shaft, and a well-marked horizontal terrace shows where the cross beam lay. It appears, from the vague indications that remain, to have been a Greek cross exactly 30m (98ft 4ins) across. Marple's plan shows the thickness of the arms as 6m (19ft 6ins), but the more detailed and persuasive Jacobs' plan made in 1923 suggests that the arms were no wider than 3m (9ft 8ins). Today the terrace is only 3.2m wide at the widest point.

Some people refer to it as the Ditchling Cross, perhaps because they have walked to it from Ditchling Beacon, but Plumpton is the nearest village and it is in Plumpton parish, so Plumpton Cross is a better name.

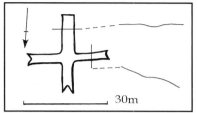

Plan made by Jacob in 1923.

There is no memory or even folk memory of the Plumpton Cross having been seen as a white cross. Blaeu mentioned it 150 years ago as being visible only under certain lighting conditions, so it must have been grass-covered for a long time even then. In the circumstances, it is remarkably well-preserved and easily identifiable. It seems it has not been cleaned or recut in the last 250–300 years, and there is only one often repeated story to explain how it came into being in the first place.

Marples' sketch plan is odd in that it is suspiciously even compared with the surveyed plan made in 1923. It also shows the arms dashed, by implication less visible than the shaft, and Marples says that it is 'partially grown over'. This suggests a lack of firsthand fieldwork, as does the remark that 'the outline can sometimes be faintly seen, so it is said, under favourable lighting conditions.' If the cross was only occasionally visible, it must have been grassed over. Marples was clearly writing from Blaeu rather than from personal observation. His two photos of the Bledlow Cross show that partially grassed over, so perhaps he was confusing his notes on the two sites.

The level terraces marking the arms suggest that from below they would have been difficult if not impossible to see, while the shaft would have been very conspicuous.

On 14 May 1924 a number of Sussex dignitaries gathered on Plumpton Plain to unveil a memorial built in the centre of the Cross by the Brighton and Hove Archaeological Club. A local historian, Frederick Harrison, made a speech about the Battle of Lewes, which had taken place exactly 660 years earlier, on 14 May 1264. Harrison said:

'. . . those who ask what evidence there is for connecting this cross with a battle, I will say at once – direct evidence, none; indirect evidence and tradition, yes. I wonder whether those who put the question are aware that there is doubt whether the place-name, Mount Harry [the next hill to the east], has any connection with the battle.'

Doubts there certainly were. Mount Harry might have derived its name from Henry III, who led one of the armies in the battle, but it is more likely that it is derived from the Old English 'harrow', which in turn came from Anglo-Saxon '*hearg*', a pagan temple. Since shrines and temples were often built on raised sites, there are several Harrow Hills, including one in the Downs north of Worthing. Mount Harry above Lewes probably had its name long before the medieval battle.

Harrison continued:

> 'Tradition says that this great cross was cut by the monks of the Priory of St Pancras, Lewes, to perpetuate the memory of those who fell in the Battle of Lewes, and to invoke the prayers of all for the repose of their souls. If this is correct, whilst the cross was kept clear of weeds and showed the white chalk, it must have been a conspicuous object. Such would have been its condition until the Dissolution of the Priory in 1537-8; after this, neglected and exposed to the elements, its appearance would be such as the weather-worn features now present.'

Unfortunately, there is absolutely no evidence to support this tradition, which has been repeated again and again as the explanation for the cross. It is true that there was great loss of life in the battle and it is true that a white cross was sewn onto the breasts and backs of de Montfort's men's surcoats. The white cross had been adopted by the English at the time of the Crusades, and de Montfort, in opposing Henry III, was identifying his soldiers with the Crusaders. A white cross would have been a fitting shape for a memorial to de Montfort's men, though not to those of the king. But the main problem is the location. The battle swept across the Downs from Mount Harry over Offham Hill and down towards what is now Lewes Prison. A mark cut on the steep northerly slopes of Offham Hill or Mount Harry would relate well to the battle, but not on Plumpton Plain, a full 2fi miles to the ·west of the battlefield. Mount Harry has a steep and concave north face that would have made an ideal site for such a memorial. So why would the Lewes monks have placed the memorial so far away? The idea of commemorating a battle with a chalk mark also smacks of Francis Wise and it puts the Plumpton Cross into the same category and mind-set as the Alfredian battle-victory signs that have already been discarded as unconvincing and unsatisfactory. No battle in Britain has ever been marked by a hill figure.

The Battle of Lewes explanation is advanced every time the Plumpton Cross is discussed, but only because there is no other explanation. Paul

Newman takes the line that since there is no other explanation, all that can be done is to acquiesce to local tradition. An alternative theory is needed. For this is a sad monument, both physically and intellectually neglected. In 1949 Morris Marples wrote of it: 'No one seems to have tried to unravel its history.' Fifty years on, that is still true.

It has been suggested that the Chiltern crosses were altered at some stage to turn them from pagan into Christian symbols, with arms added to an older vertical mark. It is possible that the Plumpton Cross too began as a vertical mark, as the shaft is significantly deeper than the terrace representing the cross beam. There is no other evidence that it represents a pre-Christian image. On the other hand, even when the Cross was impeccably maintained and all shining white, the vertical stroke must have been the part of the image that was visible from the foot of the hill, and was therefore a significantly more satisfactory element in the design than the cross beam.

The position of the Plumpton Cross, perched high on the escarpment directly south of Plumpton Place, suggests that it was designed to be seen from there. It may be that it was a folly, a landscape feature created to enhance the view from Plumpton Place, Streat Place or Novington Manor, and therefore ordered by some past owner of one of those houses. Its position strongly suggests a relationship with Plumpton Place, the nearest of these country seats, and the Cross is directly aligned on it, facing due north. It may be that the owners of Plumpton Place had the Cross added to the hill to improve the view from their house. This action would possibly have accompanied other improvements to the house, gardens and general surroundings. Which of the succession of owners may have instigated this improvement has to be a matter of speculation but, in the absence of any other satisfactory hypothesis, a little free-wheeling is allowed.

A member of the Mascall (or Maskell) family, who owned Plumpton Place from 1555 onwards, seems a likely contender. The Mascalls had been sitting tenants for some time, when in 1555 they were able to purchase. The new owners were progressive farmers, interested in new methods of land and livestock management. Leonard Mascall was a well-known writer and agronomist, who introduced the orange pippin to English orchards and carp to the moat of Plumpton Place. He wrote *Howe to Plant and Graffe all Sortes of Trees* and *The Government of Cattel*, in which he recommended that cattle stalls should open to the south. He was chief farrier to James I. Certainly a flurry of building work followed the Mascalls' purchase of Plumpton Place. The north wing, now the oldest surviving part of the house, bears the date 1568 and the initials of John Mascall. The west wing seems to have been added later, in about 1600. This phase of improvement may well have been accompanied by the addition of the Cross to the hill side.

The Mascall arms are blazoned : Sable, six fleur de lys Or, within a border engrailed argent – nothing here to prompt the cutting of a cross on the hill, so where did the idea of the Cross come from? The explanation may be that the Mascalls saw one or more of the Chiltern crosses while travelling and simply borrowed the idea. But there is another possibility.

The nave walls of Plumpton church as Leonard Mascall saw them were richly decorated with murals. They were later whitewashed over, presumably in the seventeenth century, and discovered again in 1867. The wall paintings included the Flight into Egypt, a Resurrection scene and an arresting image of two archangels holding up a cross. In fact, there were probably originally

five more figures, making an impressive and unique frieze of seven archangels. The style of dress worn by the figures in the paintings, in particular the angels' distinctive flamboyantly waved hems, shows that they were painted in the late fourteenth century.

The charged and striking image of a richly ornamented cross held aloft by a row of archangels, and seen every Sunday, must have become imprinted on generations of Plumpton parishioners. Perhaps this was the inspiration for the Plumpton Cross. It is even possible that the slight flaring of the ends of both the shaft and cross beam seen in the 1923 plan may have been borrowed from the decorative style of the painted cross in the church.

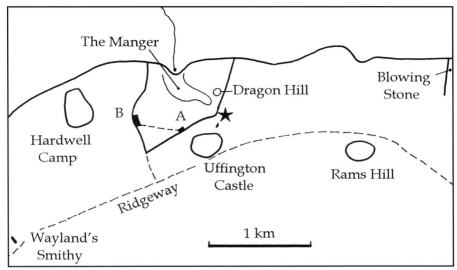

A is the small car park, B the larger one.

7

Uffington White Horse

The White Horse is huge, by far the biggest of all the British hill figures. It is 110m (360ft) long and 40m (130ft) high. Close up the image of the Horse is hard to see clearly, although its immense size can be appreciated. It is really best seen from a distance, ideally from an aeroplane or, failing that, from a train travelling between Swindon and Reading, or the car park of the Seven Stars on the Faringdon-Shrivenham road.

There is no doubt that the landscape setting of the Uffington White Horse has always been of key significance. It faces north west from near the crest of the chalk escarpment of the Berkshire Downs across

LOCATION

On the crest of the escarpment, 2fi miles south of Uffington. The B4507 runs along the foot of White Horse Hill and from it a lane branches off immediately east of Dragon Hill to a car park for the elderly and disabled. For the able-bodied there is a lane turning west of the Manger, leading to a second and larger car park. From here it is an easy and pleasant walk across sheep pasture to Uffington Castle and the Horse.

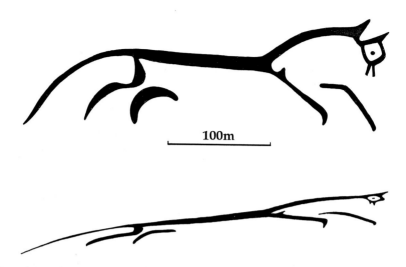

Two views of the Uffington White Horse. Above, the vertical, below, the horizontal.

a deep, steep-sided coombe called the Manger. The Saxons called the Manger *'Hringpyt'*, the Ring Pit.

To the west are some curious terraces in the scarp, known as the Giant's Stair, which were apparently created when an ice sheet butted into the hillside and disrupted the chalk strata. East of the Manger, north of the Horse's tail and near the scarp foot stands the curious isolated stump of Dragon Hill. This spur of natural rock has been shaped for some unknown purpose in antiquity. It sides have been steepened and its top levelled to make a drum shape. In the early nineteenth century Dragon Hill was thought to be a built feature such as a barrow, and the Saxons believed it was a barrow too, but when it was explored in 1852 it was concluded that it was a natural rock outcrop. Its projection well above the surrounding chalk slope nevertheless suggests that it is at least in part a built feature.

There is a bald patch on top of Dragon Hill where for some reason grass has never grown. According to Thomas Hughes there is a local tradition that this was where St George killed the dragon. Its shape suggests a ceremonial platform of some kind, and it was evidently regarded with superstition during the Roman occupation as Roman coins were found on its summit and finds of Iron Age pottery confirm that it was visited for some purpose in that period too.

It was mentioned in Saxon charters as '*Ecelesbeorg*' and must have made a distinctive boundary marker. Ninth and tenth century charters give the western boundary of Uffington parish as passing through:

> 'the top of ecelesbeorg [Dragon Hill]; from ecelesbeorg along the edge [the steep back wall of the Manger] to the barrow [probably the long barrow rather than the neighbouring bronze age round barrow north of Uffington Castle]; from the barrow into the north gate [of Uffington Castle]; thence to the south gate [right across the middle of Uffington Castle]; then out [of Uffington Castle] along the ditch [Long Ditch] to the short ditch.'

This charter displays a curious characteristic – the Saxons evidently preferred to use the barrows, ditches and banks in the area as downland markers rather than the far more conspicuous Horse. This cannot be explained entirely in terms of earthworks being more permanent, as on lower ground the boundary markers include 'bramble corner' and 'thorn tree', which were far less permanent than the Horse. Nor can the banks and barrows have been more visible than the Horse. Possibly the Saxons were silent concerning the Horse because there was some superstition or taboo relating to it. More likely, they were aware that using the Horse as a boundary

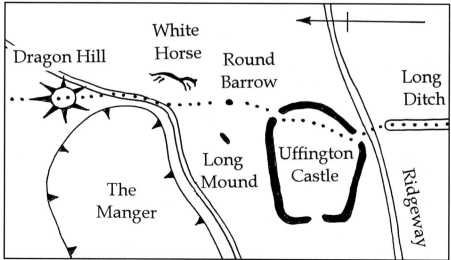

The Saxon charter boundary.

41

marker would have divided the duty of care and therefore endangered the figure's chances of being well maintained. Ensuring that the Horse was wholly and unambiguously within Uffington ensured clarity of responsibility for its upkeep.

To return briefly to Dragon Hill, which was a Saxon landmark, a narrow spur on the inner slope connects it to the escarpment, and it looks as if this was designed to give access to the circular platform from the Horse. There can be little doubt that for whatever ceremonial purpose the hill was made, it was connected in some way with the Horse.

Above the Horse and to the south, on the 152m (498ft) high summit of White Horse Hill, is the early Iron Age hillfort of Uffington Castle, which dates from 700 BC. Between the Horse and Uffington Castle is a 23m by 12m (75ft by 39ft) burial mound. This Neolithic long barrow was later re-used for forty six burials from the period of the Roman occupation. Closer still to the Horse is a Bronze Age round barrow.

The style in which the horse is drawn has excited endless discussion and argument. Some people insist that it started off semi-naturalistically, and became more stylised and abstract with successive scourings. On the other hand, comparable artwork is available on Late Iron Age coins, where the simplified, exploded image has been arrived at in one go, and there is no reason, even following David Miles' excavations, to suppose that the Horse ever looked significantly different from the way it does today. Some see it as crude, barbaric, incompetent – others as brilliantly economical, dashing, expressionistic. Certainly, when comparisons are made with other chalk horses, which show the baleful influence of George Stubbs, it is clear that the simplified, windswept lines of the Uffington Horse are more idiomatic, more suited to the medium, and more sympathetic to the landscape setting of sweeping downland.

The White Horse has the earliest documented record of all the hill figures, although even that is indirect – a mention of the hill rather than the figure. A cartulary of Abingdon Abbey from the reign of Henry II refers to a monk called Godric Cild who inherited property and was 'possessed of Spersholt, near the place commonly known as White Horse Hill.' This transaction occurred when Aldhelm was abbot, between 1072 and 1084, so it is fairly certain the Horse was on the hill by 1080. A hundred years later it was directly mentioned in Ralf de Deceto's *Tract of Wonders*:

> 'Fifth [of the Wonders] is the White Horse with his foal. It is wonderful that it was so made in the figure of a horse that over the whole place where that image of a horse is, no grass may grow. Grass never grows over the shape of the horse but always there the earth is bare to the full extent of the horse.'

The foal is something of a mystery, as no later writer mentions it. It is possible there was a second figure somewhere on the hillside, but if so no one has successfully identified it. Possibly Ralf's source listed other associated features, such as Dragon Hill or, more likely, the Manger, and Ralf made a mistake. In 1586 Camden mentioned the Vale of the White Horse rather dismissively, as named 'after some shape or other of a white horse pictured on a whitish hill.' Gough's 1806 edition of *Britannia* adds a lot of detail:

The Battle of Ashdown, drawn by Richard Doyle.

> 'The figure which gives its name to this vale is cut on a high steep hill facing the north-west, in a galloping posture, and covers near an acre of ground. His head, neck, body, tail and legs consist of one line or trench cut in the chalk about two or three feet deep and ten broad; the rays of the afternoon sun darting on it make it visible for twelve miles round at least. The neighbouring inhabitants of several villages have a custom of scouring the horse, as they call it, at certain times, about which they hold a festival, and perform certain manly games for prizes. The horse is with great probability supposed to be a memorial of Alfred's victory over the Danes at Ashdown, AD 871.'

A Saxon explanation for the Horse was popular in the nineteenth century, because the Victorians regarded the Saxons as their earliest ancestors – anything pre-Roman being seen as too alien and savage.

Francis Wise wrote briefly about the Horse, first in 1738 and again in 1742. He had heard about the custom of Scouring the Horse, was deeply impressed by the figure, and developed the idea that it was made on Alfred's orders to commemorate the Battle of Ashdown. Alfred had, after all, been born in the nearby town of Wantage in 848. But even in the nineteenth century there was dissent. Thomas Hughes, writing in 1871, expressed doubts that the Battle of Ashdown had been fought there:

'. . . nor am I sure (and this is, perhaps, greater heresy) that our White Horse was cut out on the hill after the battle. Indeed, I incline to the belief that it was there long before, and that Ethelred and Alfred could not have spent an hour on the work in the crisis of AD 871.'

During the twentieth century, the Saxon view receded, although it still had its exponents, such as Diana Woolner, who relied perhaps too much on folklore as evidence.

The idea that the Horse was a pre-Roman Celtic image gained ground, largely when comparisons were made with Iron Age coins. A Dobunnic coin was found in the fortress on the hilltop, so it may be that it was the Dobunni tribesmen who defended it, and they or their ancestors who made the Horse below it. Similar images appear on the coins of many later Iron Age tribes – stylised, serpentine, exploded horses streaking across the bronze discs. In 1929 O G S. Crawford proposed that the Uffington White Horse was the tribal emblem of the Iron Age people who created and occupied Uffington Castle. Anne Ross proposed in 1967 that the Horse stood for the major Celtic horse deity, Epona, who shared some characteristics of the goddess Rhiannon, who was often shown astride a horse, together with the key to the stable and a crescent moon.

In the Iron Age Celtic world, the horse was revered for its power, beauty, swiftness and bravery, and its sexual vigour made it a natural symbol of fertility, prosperity and well-being. Horse cults are known to have been widespread in the Iron Age, even to the extent of horse sacrifices. The horse was shown on coins, not just in Britain but in other parts of Europe too. Coins from Slovakia, for instance, showed a stylised, exploded horse accompanied by a sun wheel, which is a reminder that the Uffington Horse need not be Epona's mare but the sun god's steed. The sun god was often thought of, like Apollo, Helios or Phaeton, as driving a chariot drawn by horses across the sky. Whether these Celtic horse images all derived ultimately from the fourth century BC coins of Philip of Macedon, as is often stated, is open to question.

Conqueror of darkness, evil and death, the sun god was a sky warrior who depended on his horse for his phenomenal mobility. Sometimes he could be represented in iconography by his horse on its own. The horse on the hill may therefore not necessarily have been worshipped by its makers; they simply saw the horse as important enough to act as a substitute or emblem of the deity, in much the same way that in 1500 BC the Minoan goddess Potnia could be represented by her double axe, the god Poseidon by his bull, and later on the god-man Christ could be represented by the cross on which he died. These substitutions are common in religious art, and sometimes throw difficulties in the way of interpretation by incompletely informed people of later cultures.

Passing along the hill crest above the Horse is a major prehistoric highway, the Ridgeway. It leads south to Wayland's Smithy, a fine megalithic tomb. The legend of Wayland, the maimed Norse/Teutonic master smith, was a story told in the Saxon territories, and it attached itself to this much earlier Neolithic communal grave. The story adapted itself to the Saxon geography, with Wayland settling in the Vale, using the megalithic ruin as a smithy, and shoeing horses – including, of course, the great White Horse itself.

The Scourings of the White Horse were described in the eighteenth century, and must have gone on, probably at irregular intervals rather than the proverbial 'every seven years', for at least 800 years before that. The *Reading Mercury* reported in March 1789 that 'the White Horse on the side of the downs, in White Horse Vale, has been lately recut so that at a distance of three or four miles, it is perhaps one of the most lively representations of an elegant shaped Horse, except that the Horse's back. . . is rather too long.'

A few years earlier, in 1782, that newspaper reported that:

'The White Horse was cleaned for many years by William, Lord Barrington, but the ground on which the horse is cut being allotted by the Commissioners of the Uffington Inclosure, 1775, to William, Lord Craven, his lordship has since that time cleansed it annually at his expense, and has twice celebrated the Scouring of the Horse with every country diversion, at which sports there were computed to be 30,000 spectators'.

In 1892 the Horse was scoured, apparently without festivities, under the direction of Andrew Dudgeon of Uffington, by order of Lady Craven. The work cost £10.

There is archaeological evidence of a fair of some kind being held in

Uffington Castle in the late Roman period. The Uffington 'pastime', as it was called, is vigorously documented in Thomas Hughes' 1857 book, *The Scouring of the White Horse.* In 1720, Thomas Cox noted 'a custom, once a year, at or near Midsummer, to go and weed it in order to keep the Horse in shape and colour; and after the work is over they end the day in feasting and merriment.' Wise mentions that the games had lost much of their 'ancient splendour', by which it is assumed he means that people were having a good time and not standing on their dignity. The 'good belly-full of ale' mentioned by Wise's contemporary, William Asplin, confirms as much. The games included competitions such as sack races, cheese rolling and cudgel-playing for a gold laced hat and a pair of pumps. A contest introduced in 1808 invited ladies to compete in a pipe-smoking marathon. Hughes noted that 'only two gipsy women entered'; the prize was half a guinea or – probably more necessary in the circumstances – a gallon of gin.

A late ballad re-affirmed the place of Alfred in all this:

> The Old White Horse wants setting to rights
> And the Squire has promised good cheer;
> So we'll give him a scrape to keep him in shape,
> And he'll last for many a year.

> He was made a long, long time ago
> With a great deal of labour and pains,
> By King Alfred the Great, when he spoiled their conceit,
> And caddled they worsbirds the Danes.

'Caddled' is Berkshire dialect for 'harassed'; 'worsbird' means 'whore's bird', or, groping for a modern paraphrase, something like 'son of a bitch'.

The pastime seems always to have been a two-day event, generally held within the earthworks of Uffington Castle. There were booths, tents, sideshows, with a platform for wrestling and backsword play. According to Hughes, 'Every show had its own music, if it were only a drum and pan-pipes, and all the musicians were playing different tunes.'

There were pastimes, and therefore scourings, in 1755, 1765, 1776, 1780, 1785, 1789, 1796,1803, 1813, 1825, 1838, 1843 and in 1857, which was the last time a pastime was held. From the dates given by Hughes and Plenderleath, it does not look as if the scourings took place at regular seven year intervals.

In 1880 the Horse was reported to be 'so overgrown with weeds as scarcely to be discernible from a distance'.It was scoured four years later and then again in 1892, 1908 and 1914. More recently, ironically, the cleaning has been less well documented.

A nineteenth century scouring of the Horse.

The White Horse had to be covered up during the Second World War as it was too good a way-mark for German bomber pilots heading for Coventry. After the war, it was uncovered and cleaned under the super-vision of W F Grimes, who took the opportunity in 1952 to dig a test pit in the Horse's curious beak. It was a surprise to discover that the visible chalk was not the solid chalk and that the outline had been created by digging a deep trench through the soil and the slopewash which here covers the solid chalk, and then filled up to the level of the grass with chalk rubble. No action was taken in response to Grimes's report to the Ministry of Works, although the many laminations of chalky silt Grimes's pit penetrated implied that the figure had been recut and refilled many times.

It was not until the 1990s that the site and the ideas that it generated were revisited by archaeologists. David Miles and Simon Palmer saw from Grimes's report that the Horse could, potentially, be dissected. The fact that it was built onto the hillside made it possible to extract some sort of narra-tive of the figure's development. The beak pit was reopened, and Miles and Palmer found the outline to be a metre deep, with some of the layers of fill extending more than a metre further down the slope than the modern beak lines. Trenching across the horse's belly, which Diana Woolner believed had once been much fuller, revealed that the body was indeed originally wider, but only by about a metre. The outline was never, it seems, signifi-cantly different from the way it looks today. The slope of the figure, how-ever, has changed. With each rebuilding and subsequent weathering phase, the chalky surface of the figure has become eroded at the upper edge and the chalk silt produced has accumulated at the lower edge. Over long periods of time this has led to the raising of the lower edge and the tilting of the image up towards the sky; it has becomes correspondingly more difficult to see it clearly from below.

The most spectacular results of David Miles' research were undoubtedly the Optically Stimulated Luminescence Dates (OSL) obtained from the lowest layers of silt. This new technique measures the length of time a buried soil or silt has been shut away from the sunlight. The three dates produced a range 1400–600 BC, showing that the figure was probably made in the late Bronze Age or earliest Iron Age. David Miles believes the later end of the range is more likely, as there was a lot of other activity in the area around 700 BC, such as the creation of the big earthwork enclosures of Uffington Castle and Ramsbury, a short distance to the east along the Ridgeway. Marples suggested that 'the Uffington Horse is much older than even Wise supposed, possibly of Early Iron Age date': this is Miles' conclusion too, but based on a scientific dating method.

The Horse cannot have been cut later than the earliest surviving silt layer, which means that these OSL dates give the latest date by which it was tethered on White Horse Hill. The early date of the White Horse has caused an adjustment in thinking in several areas. Many people assumed from the similarity between the chalk image and the horse images on late Iron Age coins that the hill figure had to belong to the Late Iron Age *La Tene* culture. Now it appears that images taken to be *La Tene* were made long before that culture existed.

The kinship with the images on late Iron Age coins is striking, even to the peculiar beak. The curious and so far unexplained double-stroked forked tongue pointing downwards from the horse's chin is not just a local feature – it appears on the late Iron Age silver coin, pictured left, from Slovakia.

Another fact that has been established is that for the past 1,700 years the people of the area have been going up regularly – on average every ten to twenty years – to remake the figure. That in itself gives an astonishing insight into the strength of local customs, and reinforces the idea that folklore and oral history traditions may be longer-lived than was thought possible.

The Horse may have been put here in the first place because it was a major socio-political boundary. The crest of the escarpment was a frontier in the early Iron Age; the late Bronze Age/early Iron Age Grims Ditch follows it for 9 miles, about half the distance between the White Horse and the Thames. Other, apparently contemporary, v-shaped ditches run from north to south from the Ridgeway down the crests of spurs, presumably bounding valley farms, and one of them runs south from Uffington Castle.

The White Horse was at the meeting place of four Late Iron Age tribal territories – the Catuvellauni to the north east, the Atrebates to the south east, North Dobunni to the north west and South Dobunni to the south west and must have made an effective tribal boundary marker at that time. The area was a busy one at this period with the Ridgeway in use as frontier highway, fortified enclosures like Uffington Castle, known to the Saxons as 'Ashbury', and nearby Ramsbury, the Saxon 'Ravensbury', built beside it and another enclosure, Hardwell Camp, created at the scarp foot. Whether the spring at the bottom of the Manger was accorded cult status is not known, but it is certainly possible that this was an early iron age religious site. The Saxon charters refer to it only as the 'riverhead'. The discovery at Uffington of an Etruscan statuette, evidently imported by a wealthy chief in the fifth century BC, shows Uffington as a focus for an ambitious, high-status community in the middle Iron Age. On the south east flank of White Horse Hill a bronze stud enamelled in red, also Iron Age in date, was found.

Perhaps the oddest feature of the Uffington White Horse is that it was built on the relatively gentle 20° slope of a Bronze Age cultivation terrace, which makes it rather difficult to see clearly from below. If the Horse had been drawn just 20m lower, it would have been on a slope twice as steep and been an even more spectacular landscape feature, easily visible from the Vale below. But perhaps there was some symbolic or ritual reason, now long forgotten, for creating it on old, abandoned farmland.

8

Red Horse of Tysoe

This horse has long since bolted, well before the age of photography and unfortunately there are few reliable drawings or descriptions of it. The site, at Edgehill on the steep north west facing escarpment of the Cotswolds, is now covered with mature trees, since its deliberate afforestation in 1959, an act which is hard to forgive since the figure is now beyond recovery. However, some work was done before the trees took over and it is possible to reconstruct the design on paper. From the bridle-way it is possible to gain a fair impression of the site – a uniform forty degree slope which is ideal for hill figure construction – and assess the level of post-war destruction inflicted on it. The roots of the mature

LOCATION.

From the A422 Banbury-Stratford road turn south just west of Upton House onto the minor road that runs southwards along the crest of the escarpment. After about half a mile, park on the roadside and take the path way-marked Centenary Way. This passes into a wood called The Hangings and goes diagonally down the escarpment. The wood itself is private land and there is no right of access to the hill figure.

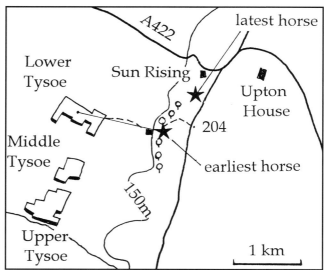

closed woodland of beech, ash, larch and sycamore have disrupted much of the buried outline, and badger setts will have destroyed the little that remains. There was a sequence of horses, replacing one another, suggesting that scouring, as at Uffington, was not frequently or systematically carried out, and that the image was from time to time lost under weeds and grass and had to be redrawn. The successive images were evidently significantly different from each other. The latest was the northernmost, cut at Sun Rising, Grid Reference 359458, between the belt of woodland and the crest of the ridge.

An eighteenth century engraving from the Aylesford Collection of Warwickshire drawings in Birmingham Reference Library shows the horse walking elegantly, with two legs straight and one foreleg and one back leg raised. It had a saddle and stirrup, but no rider. This horse was short-lived, and ploughed over in 1800. There was an earlier image, which was celebrated in the seventeenth century, and this was well to the south at 353458. Some reports suggest 355452 or among the trees at the spring a kilometre further south at 353443. But the location in The Hangings at 353458 has been authenticated by resistivity surveys and photographs.

The Red Horse of Tysoe, after a sepia sketch in the Aylesford Collection.

In 1612, the poet Michael Drayton used the Red Horse as a symbol of his own neglected state as a writer, while the White Horse of Uffington has all the fame:

> White Horse . . . is exalted to the skies,
> My Red Horse of you all contemned lies,
> The fault is not in me, but in the wretched time,
> On whom, upon good cause, I may well lay the crime,
> Which as all noble things, so mee it does neglect.

Drayton evidently expected his readers to know of the Red Horse and, presumably, to realise that the figure was overgrown or poorly maintained, although it may have been only relatively so, by comparison with the much-acclaimed White Horse. The cartographer Speed refers to Red Horse Vale in 1606, and the horse itself was mentioned in the following year by Camden, who wrote, 'a great part of the very vale is termed the Vale of the Red Horse, of the shape of the horse cut out in a red hill by the country people hard by Pillerton'.

Later in the seventeenth century, Sir William Dugdale described the horse in more detail. In 1642 he fought beside Charles I at the Battle of Edgehill, possibly within sight of the Red Horse – the battle was just three miles to the north – but he must have returned later to study it under quieter conditions. In 1656 he wrote:

'There is cut in the side of Edgehill the proportion of a horse in very large forme; which by reason of the ruddy colour of the earth is called the Red Horse, and giveth denomination to that fruitful and pleasant country thereabouts called the Vale of the Red Horse: the trenches of which ground where the shape of the said horse is so cut out, being yearly scoured by a Free-holder in this lordship who holds certain lands there by that service'.

Dugdale's report reveals that not only was the Red Horse maintained in the seventeenth century, but it was somebody's specific duty to maintain it. He declared the Red Horse to be 'a very large forme.' If that was so, it is hard to understand why Francis Wise, writing in 1742, dismissed it in a few words as 'vastly inferior to the Uffington Horse.' He may have been considering the Red Horse's age – much younger, he thought – and artistry – clumsy and inept – rather than its size. Richard Gough's description of 1806 is much harder to explain away, as it contains measurements. From rump to chest it was 34ft long, from shoulder to ground 16ft, while the tail, 'more like a lion's', was 18ft. This was a small hill figure by comparison with Uffington, and does not seem to be the same beast described in Richard Jago's poem:

The Red Horse drawn to Gough's measurements.

And Tysoe's wondrous theme, the martial Horse,
Carved on the yielding turf, armorial sign
Of Hengist, Saxon chief! Studious to preserve

The fav'rite form, the treach'rous conquerors,
Their vassal tribes compel with festive rites
Its fading figure yearly to renew
And to the neighb'ring vale impart its name.

Here is the almost inevitable Saxon explanation for the hill figure, but, more interestingly, a repetition of the idea that it was weeded annually. Some of the difficulties may disperse when it is realised that the eighteenth century horse was a replacement for the one seen by Dugdale and Drayton. The older Horse faced north, while the newer and smaller one seen by Wise and Gough faced south.

Research by K Carrdus and W Miller pointed towards a location on The Hangings for the older horse. Photographs of this site show an area of paler grass the shape of a huge galloping horse. In style it was halfway between the genteel modern horse of the Aylesford engraving and the explosively free expressionism of the Uffington Horse. This pale patch was nearly 90 metres long and 64 metres high. That is huge, and on a similar scale to the Uffington figure. Accompanying the giant horse was another, 'two-thirds the size of the first', which looked like a foal galloping ahead of its mother. North, ie in front, of this was another pale area suggesting a third, smaller creature about 16 metres long. This may not have been part of the original image or it may represent the late seventeenth or early eighteenth century replacement, the one Wise regarded as inferior.

This inferior horse was the one that was destroyed by ploughing in the late eighteenth century. The proprietor of the Sunrising Inn, Simon Nicholls, bought Sunrising Farm from the Marquess of Northampton and seems to have felt no obligation to continue to maintain the Horse. However, losing the custom of the Palm Sunday horse-scourers made him think again, and he cut yet another horse as a waymark for his inn. This was regarded as even more inferior than the last, and it too became grassed over.

In 1971 S G Wildman's book about Tysoe was published. Wildman started off by trying to find the Red Horse and the site he looked at seems to have been the one in The Hangings, where small trees had already covered the slope. He reasoned that plants would grow more readily where the soil was deeper and decided that measurements of tree height would reveal the shape of the hill figure. Several months of measurements produced the outlines of two elongated horse-like shapes.

Then came an offer of air photographs. On these, he was convinced he could see not only a horse but a 48 metre high giant man waving a whip, as well as two more indistinct forms. This extraordinary mural frieze of gods and mythic incidents, which would have no parallel anywhere else, was thought to show Tiw displaying his mastery over the horse. The accompanying goose was an attribute of the corpse of the slaughtered beast underneath.

Possibly Wildman did stumble on two of the several horse images cut on the escarpment. There may have been two horses on Spring Hill. The other forms Wildman thought he could deduce are hard to believe in, not least because they are stylistically inconsistent, even with one another, and do not fit the iconography of any known period or culture.

Two resistivity surveys have been undertaken on the hillside, one by J S Stanley in 1967 and the other in 1980 by C Heathcote. Areas of high resistivity indicating disturbed ground corresponded well with the areas showing as pale green on the 1964 photographs. Prolonged exposure of the soil where the grass had been removed would lead to soil compaction, reduced water-holding capacity and probably account for the raised resistivity.

The 1967 resistivity survey was followed in 1969 by a small scale excavation. Two trial trenches were dug, across neck and ear and traces of a buried outline trench cut over half a metre deep into the red clay were found. There were also traces of 'a rather brighter red silt' lining the figure suggesting that red silt was deliberately spread across the outline to make it stand out more sharply. The second survey was said to show two horse-like figures, the mare and the foal, 'the one possibly overlapping the other.' This detail seems to show that the two horses were probably not intended to be part of the same image, but were two successive images.

The resistivity survey results should be treated with caution. They do not show clear images of anything at all. Anyone not expecting to find horses on the plan displaying the results would never infer them from the irregular image. There are smudges of high resistivity associated with the massive body of the oldest horse, the Great Horse, and the smaller horses in front of it, but their edges are irregular. It is also possible to infer two extra linear anomalies. One of these is above and behind the Great Horse and may represent the tail of an earlier or later horse. The other is a shorter curved line below and in front, and this may indicate the leg of another horse. So there

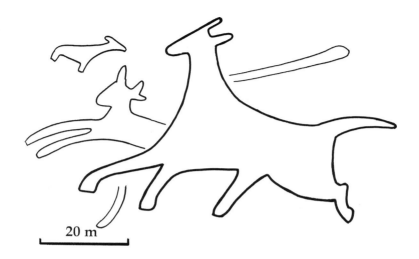

The Red Horse inferred from resistivity surveys.

may be hints in the geophysical survey results that there were as many as five successive horses in The Hangings.

It seems unlikely, now the site has been covered with woodland, that much more can be learnt about it. The development of penetrative root systems will have made any future geophysical survey, with whatever refinements are made to those techniques, impossible.

Ralf de Deceto, in his *Tract of Wonders,* mentioned that the Uffington White Horse had a foal, which it almost certainly did not. This is puzzling, unless we suppose that in Ralf's time there was another hill figure showing a horse which did have a foal, and that Ralf was simply mixing the two sites up. Although not proof of the antiquity of the Red Horse, the fact that there was talk of a 'mare-and-foal' hill figure in the twelfth century does suggest that the Red Horse group existed at that time. The antiquity of the Red Horse is not proved. It was on the hill by the first decade of the seventeenth century and we may suspect from Ralf de Deceto's slip that it was there in the twelfth too. But was it there much before that?

The place name may hold a clue. Tysoe means 'spur or scarp belonging to Tiw'. Tiw was the Teutonic Mars, a Saxon protector-god who was a powerful warrior in time of war and a patron of agricultural production in time of peace. Tacitus reminds us that the Germans sacrificed prisoners to Mars (Tiw) and Mercury (Woden), and it may be that ceremonies involving sacrifices took place on or beneath, or even above, the hill figure.

March was the month dedicated by the Romans to Mars, and Palm Sunday was the appointed time for the horse of Tiw to be cleaned. The Romans held a racing festival for Mars on March 14, which is not far from the (movable) Christian feast of Palm Sunday. The landscape setting may also be significant since hills near at hand are named Spring and Sunrising. The spring reference is more likely to be to the many stream sources to be found at high altitudes on the escarpment rather than to the season.

If the creation and initial usage of the Horse were associated with Tiw, the figure would have been made by the Angles, who settled in the Stour valley in around 600, and could therefore date from 600–700. An association with Tiw and the allocation of the name Tysoe could all have come after the creation of the figure, and it may turn out to be older still.

At Uffington, there is an early Iron Age figure possibly representing the steed of the sun god or the goddess Epona. Did the Tysoe Horse come from the same stable? Support comes from a Gaulish relief, pictured left, showing the goddess Epona sitting on a high-stepping mare with a foal frisking about between her legs. On another carving from Burgundy, the foal trots behind, its head raised in the hope of being fed. The inclusion of the foal may be a reminder of the horse as a fertility or life-force symbol.

Significantly, the Tysoe figure seems to have had a foal. Whether the several horses at Tysoe were successive images or were drawn two at a time is difficult to tell, but the isolated reference to the Uffington Horse having a foal may well be a glimpse of the pairing of mare and foal in an Iron Age image at Tysoe.

Interest in hill figures has grown steadily during the twentieth century, and here is a case of that interest actually bringing about the destruction of a figure. The grassed-over remains of the various versions of the Red Horse were deliberately destroyed by the owner, who is alleged to have planted trees over it because he was irritated by visitors coming to see it. Is a reconstruction possible? Probably the best that can be done is to collect the evidence of the geophysical surveys and air photographs.

The oldest horse is probably the biggest, and its size – equivalent to that of the Uffington White Horse – and free expressionistic style, both suggest an Iron Age date. There is little in the way of archaeological context to help. There are no traces of barrows or earthworks on the flat crest of the hill and no signs of a prehistoric settlement or sanctuary below. There is an Iron Age fort, Nadbury Camp, three miles away to the north at Edgehill, and there was an settlement near it, also on the scarp crest near Ratley at 357457. Between the two a section of the ridge, Knowle End, was marked off by a linear barrier, probably as a ceremonial area. The Red Horse of Tysoe could have functioned as a waymark for the major Iron Age site at Nadbury but, if so, there seems no compelling reason why it should have been misplaced.

A possible explanation is that the horse indicated that there was a way up onto the escarpment at Tysoe, and there was indeed a spur road leading up from the Fosse Way during the Roman occupation immediately to the south of the Horse. The Horse would have been visible from the Fosse Way. It was shown galloping northwards, perhaps to indicate that this was the way to travel once the scarp crest road had been gained.

The road along the top of the ridge probably follows a prehistoric track-way, which gives the site a point in common with Cerne, Wilmington and Uffington. Although not marked on the Ordnance Survey map, there is a spring at Old Lodge Farm, with a stream flowing north westwards down a shallow valley. The spring is directly beneath the site of the Horse and may have been a cult focus, like the spring at Cerne Abbas. The Ordnance Survey map also shows a track leading up to Red Horse Hill from Lower Tysoe. This would have been the access road from the village to the Red Horse and also to Old Lodge Farm. Both the road and the two cottages beside it have virtually disappeared as completely as the Red Horse to which it led. Access to Old Lodge Farm is now by a private drive dropping down the escarpment.

The location of the last Horse, near Sunrising Hill.

The thickly wooded site of the Great Horse of Tysoe. Left of centre is one of the derelict cottages beside the abandoned farm track.

The village of Tysoe was held by a Saxon chief called Waga before the Norman conquest, when it was known as Tiheshoche. In the Middle Ages it had weekly markets and a major Lammas Fair lasting four days. It was common for such fairs to feature festivities associated with traditions of the locality, and these may have included the Red Horse. One local belief was that the Horse commemorated the action of Richard Neville, Warwick 'The Kingmaker', at the Battle of Towton on Palm Sunday, 1461, when he is said to have killed his own horse as a sign that he was not going to leave the battlefield. There has for a long time been a feeling among scholars that the Horse is in reality much older.

In the twelfth century, some of the Tysoe lands were granted to the Knights Templars, who had some kind of centre at Lower Tysoe, the hamlet that lies directly in front of the Horse, and which consequently became known as Temple Tysoe. Whether the Red Horse held any special interest or attraction for the Templars is not known. Whether the people of Tysoe, Upper, Middle or Lower, had any special interest in the Red Horse is not known either. What is known is that it was a village where witchcraft, or at least an unusually strong belief in witchcraft, prevailed, and to a surprisingly late date. In the early nineteenth century there were reports of assaults on women believed to be witches, and a case of an old woman showing great reluctance to use a walking stick because it was a sure sign of a witch.

Tysoe church has fourteenth century corbels showing a range of non-Christian images. One is a classic Green Man image of a human face spouting leaves, and a semi-human face with long ears. Another, a bearded man with his tongue sticking out, is a frightener of the sort seen at Cerne Abbas. Another shows a grotesque beast that may be a spotted leopard. Not too much should be read into these images, however, as many medieval churches had these pre-Christian or extra-Christian symbols built into them without any hill figure associations.

9

The Cerne Giant

This well-preserved figure is the outline of a naked man 55 metres tall walking northwards along the hillside and waving a knobbly club 37 metres long above his bald and earless head. He wears nothing but a belt –which no one notices – and a considerable amount of other detail is shown within the outline including his fingers, eyes, eyebrows, mouth, nipples, pectoral muscles, ribs, testicles and 7 metre phallus – which everyone notices. The details of the figure are interesting, and beautifully maintained by the National Trust warden, William Keighley. The

LOCATION.

On the steep west fac-
ing slope of Giant Hill,
half a kilometre north
of Cerne Abbas. There
is an official viewpoint
in a layby in the slip
road leading from the
A352 into Cerne Abbas.
Although there is a
footpath from there to
the Giant, it is not
worth going any nearer
because the figure can-
not be seen properly
from close to.
The site is surrounded
by a substantial fence
and there is no public
access to it. For the
sake of conservation,
the fence should be
respected.

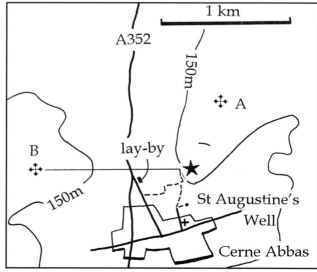

A is the Iron Age farmstead on Giant Hill, B the one on Weam Common Hill.

overall aspect is warlike and menacing. The right arm is raised, waving the huge club. The left trails aimlessly, leading many to suggest that something now lost was once held in the left hand.

The outline is a neatly edged trench that appears to be 40cm wide and cut through soil only 10–15cm (4-6ins) deep to expose the chalk bedrock. Probably from the beginning the trench was lined with fresh, unweathered chalk from elsewhere to get a uniform whiteness. The original drawing would not have been difficult to create, but digging 25 tonnes of chalk from nearly half a kilometre of trenches involved a significant amount of work. Today the trench is filled right up to the level of the grass with compacted chalk rubble, to make the image plainly visible from the valley floor below and to stop rain water eroding and distorting it. This was probably the prehistoric method for making hill figures. They were as much built as cut.

Photographs of the Cerne Giant in the 1930s show the outlines as grassed trenches, largely emptied of their fill, with a narrow line of chalk visible at the bottom. This development is interesting in view of the Long Man of Wilmington's appearance in the eighteenth and nineteenth centuries as a Green Giant.

The eighteenth century Dorset historian, the Reverend John Hutchins, visited Cerne Abbas in about 1750 and was dined by the vicar, who told him of a tradition, current among his parishioners, that a giant 'resided hereabouts in former ages, the pest and terror of the adjacent country.' The giant went off into the Vale of Blackmore, gobbled up a flock of sheep and then dozed off on the hillside at Cerne. The local people seized their opportunity, pinned him to the ground, killed him where he lay and afterwards traced the outlined of his murdered corpse to commemorate the event.

Thomas Hardy heard a more sinister strand of giant lore:

'. . . he threatened to descend upon Cerne and to ravish all the young maidens on a particular night and kill the young men the next day'.

Hardy refers to the Giant again in *The Dynasts*:

'They say he [Napoleon] lives upon human flesh and has rashers of baby for breakfast – for all the world like the Cernel Giant in old ancient times'.

Others notice that the Giant's phallus points due east, where the sun rises on the 'true' horizon at the equinoxes. On the other hand, 21 March and 21 September seem not to have been celebrated as major festivals in the Iron Age calendar. It may be, as still others have pointed out, that the sun rises over Giant Hill in line with the phallus on May Morning, because the local horizon, the crest of the hill, is significantly higher than the true horizon. The vantage point from which this sunrise was viewed is not at all obvious, so the arguments are in the end elusive and unconvincing.

The story that at sunset the Giant slips down to the River Cerne for a drink and to catch and eat unwary virgins is far more appealing, though I have lingered there at dusk and seen nothing.

The folklore relating to fertility and pregnancy is understandable, given the figure's sexual emphasis, but it was not mentioned at all until 1888. It is said that girls and women who fear losing their boyfriends or husbands come and walk round the Giant to keep their partners' interest. Women about to marry used to visit the Giant as a normal part of preparation for marriage. Married women are said to have sat on the phallus to ensure pregnancy; couples wanting children are said to have had sex on the phallus to make sure. Such claims are still made.

There is a strong local belief that the Giant is ancient, and the thrust of my own research supports that view, but it is currently fashionable among academics to present him as a seventeenth century cartoon so, given the climate of the times, it is necessary to review the evidence with care.

The earliest definitive, unambiguous documentary reference to the Cerne Giant is a churchwardens' account dated November 1694, which tells of a repair out of parish funds: 'for repaireing of ye Giant 3s 0d.'

There is a probable earlier oblique reference in the 1660s in the anonymous *A Fool's Bolt soon shott at Stonage.* This is thought to have been written by Robert Gay, rector of Nettlecombe from 1631 to 1672, and since it includes a reference to ideas in Inigo Jones's *Stonehenge Restored,* published in 1655, it is likely to have been written in the 1660s. The passage describes a battle fought on Salisbury Plain in ancient times and won by 'the illustrious Stanengs and his Cangick giants from k. Divitiacus and his Belgae'. 'Cangick' is probably intended to be 'Cerngick' and the writer evidently knew of a giant or giants at Cerne, so the hill figure must have existed in the 1660s.

The lack of unambiguous documentation earlier than 1694 has led Dr Joe Bettey, Professor Ronald Hutton, Jeremy Harte and others to argue that the Giant was created not long before, in the seventeenth century. In fact, Leslie Grinsell and Joe Bettey argued in 1980–81 that Francis Wise's description of the Giant in 1742 was the oldest documentary reference and that the Giant must therefore have been made not long before that date. Vivian Vale's subsequent discovery of the Giant reference in the 1694 accounts necessarily pushed the Giant's latest possible date back fifty years, and at a stroke illustrated the fundamental weakness of Grinsell's and Bettey's line of reasoning. A further chance discovery of the same type could push the Giant's date back another fifty years, or 500. Too much is made to depend on the absence of evidence, when it is known that a great many documents have perished with the passage of time, and a great many elements of the English landscape were in any case never written about. Francis Wise was aware of this:

> 'The White Horse is an antiquity of a class that had hitherto [ie until his earlier letter of 1739] escaped the observation of the curious . . . a noble but hitherto neglected monument of antiquity.'

Robert Gay, in *A Fool's Bolt,* similarly writes that:

> 'Gildas of Bathe, within 20 miles of Stonage, writing in AD 543, hath not a word of it, nor venerable Bede, who writing *anno* 727 of many other rarities of this land, hath not a word of Stonage, nor William of Malms-burie, writing *anno* 1142, within 14 miles of Stonage, hath not a word of it.'

Obviously, Stonehenge existed all along, even though these historians failed to report it.

But there is a strong lobby for a seventeenth origin for the Giant, which must be examined. When Hutchins dined at Cerne Abbas in 1750, another of the supper guests was the lord of the manor's steward. After listening to the clerics' views on the Giant as a great antiquity, the steward said he knew that the Giant was recently made as a lampoon aimed at Lord Holles, who lived at Cerne Abbas, and cut by Lord Holles's servants after they killed his son in about 1660. The reference to a scouring in 1694 is consistent with an initial cutting in about 1660, although equally consistent with a much earlier origin.

Holles was certainly a controversial politician, a Parliamentarian who changed sides to play a leading role in restoring the monarchy. He had enemies, but it is hard to see how the Cerne Giant would have been an appropriate lampoon. A cartoon of Holles as presiding judge holding the scales of justice, or an axe or gallows, to mark his deserved punishment as a traitor, would have made sense. He could have been decapitated. But why show him naked, with erect penis and waving a club? And why would this childish slight be necessary if his servants had just murdered his son? This local fakelore is unconvincing. It almost goes without saying that Holles's son was not murdered. Francis Holles went on to become the second Baron Holles and MP for Dorchester in 1679.

The mid-eighteenth century steward's story may even so have contained a half-truth. Vivian Vale has suggested that the figure may have been cut by unruly servants while Holles was out of the country, mainly it seems for his own safety, in 1651. His wife wrote to him saying that the estate at Cerne was being neglected by the steward, Lamb. There was a further period of uncertain control when Lady Holles died and the inheritance of the estate was disputed and this would have created further opportunities for the citizens of Cerne Abbas to behave badly, although it seems unlikely that anyone would invest so much work in a project unless ordered or paid to do it. Vale has nevertheless discovered this period of squirearchical instability at Cerne, which explains why the church took on the responsibility for organising and paying for cleaning the Giant when it became necessary in 1694. It also explains why there was no earlier mention of the Giant in the churchwardens' accounts. On all other occasions, as eighteenth century observers have commented, it had been the lord of the manor's responsibility.

The steward who spoke to Hutchins was probably referring not to the creation of the Giant in Lord Holles's time, but to a recutting in the 1660s. It is easy to imagine that in the political turmoil of the 1640s and 1650s the repair of the figure may have been deferred, and that in his secure retirement years Holles may have overseen a thorough clean up. But that does not mean, as Harte has attempted to argue, that the Giant was created just thirty years before that. An origin in the 1630s is unlikely, as the Cerne Abbas maypole was destroyed in a surge of puritanism in 1635.

Recently, a lot of press publicity has been given to Bettey's theory that the Giant is a cartoon of Oliver Cromwell, on the basis that Cromwell was seen as a latter-day Hercules and the Giant is waving what looks like a Herculean club. There is absolutely nothing to connect Cromwell with Cerne. It would, moreover, have been extraordinary for a seventeenth century artist to design a political cartoon that in total and to every last detail has all the characteristics of a piece of Iron Age artwork. The coincidence would be too incredible.

The case for an Iron Age origin for the Cerne Giant is strong. All the various features of the drawing can be found in British and European artwork from the period 600BC to AD200. The nakedness of the Giant, which some people find disturbing or amusing, was characteristic of many Iron Age Celtic tribesmen, who often went into battle naked. Polybius said of the Gaesatae at the Battle of Telamon in 225 BC, that they:

'discarded their clothes and stood naked with nothing but their arms in front of the whole array, thinking that thus they would be more efficient, as some of the ground was overgrown with brambles that would catch in their clothes' .

In 50 BC Diodorus added another detail:
'Some [of the Celts] so despise death that they descend to do battle unclothed except for a girdle'.

The Giant, too, wears nothing but a girdle, which means that he is either about to do battle or returning triumphant from battle. Archaeology supports these descriptions of the classical writers. A Slovenian figurine made in about 500BC shows a warrior naked but for a helmet and a belt.

A sandstone statue, pictured right, from Hirschlanden in Germany, also made in about 500BC, shows a helmeted but otherwise naked warrior wearing a torc round his neck and a belt round his waist. There is a dagger stuck through the belt, which shows that the girdle described by Diodorus had a simple, practical function. Examples could be multiplied, but the nudity and the girdle together strongly suggest a Celtic warrior from the Middle or Late Iron Age. The Giant's face is equally consistent with an Iron Age origin. It is a face seen again and again in carvings – smooth, oval, hairless, earless, with round staring eyes, straight nose and expressionless mouth. The drawing of the nipples and navel were as circles, typical of Celtic art. The provocative display of genitals is common in Iron Age art, but it is a mistake to jump to the conclusion that this proves a fertility cult. The vaginal display seen in the later sheela-na-gigg carvings is not intended to be erotic; indeed the repulsiveness of the hag-like images was a deliberate ploy to ward off evil. Similarly, male genital display was intended to frighten rather than excite.

Sexual gestures and expletives have always had, and still have, widespread use as a shorthand for 'get out' or 'go away'. The Giant's erection shows him frightening off his tribe's enemies. He is protecting the territory with his penis. The huge size of the Giant's phallus is often cited as proof of a fertility link, but it was lengthened relatively recently. During the 1908 scouring, it seems the workmen ran the sides of the phallus up into the ring of the navel, and this error – or practical joke – has never been corrected. The original phallus was 4.5 metres not 7 metres long, the length *not* exaggerated in relation to the rest of the figure.

The phallus was a recurring image in the Iron Age world, on statues, cult images, pottery and amulets. Phallus amulets gave protection against destructive forces, and they were routinely carried by Roman soldiers. The Roman attitude, the Iron Age European attitude in general, was different from the prevailing attitude to the phallus in modern Europe. Augustus, for instance, called Horatius, whom he greatly respected, 'my very best penis'.

The club suggests a man who could not afford a sword. Resistivity surveys I undertook in 1989–95 showed that the ground under the outstretched left arm had been disturbed, and it looks as there were once two extra lines snaking down from the Giant's armpit and up again to the left wrist. These look like a cloak draped over the left arm and hanging down ten metres from it. What was this for? If the Giant owned a cloak, why was he not wearing it?

The answer is given by several Iron

The Giant restored, based on resistivity and close contour surveys.

66

Age artworks, such as the Gaulish bronze figurines made in the first century BC. These show naked warriors wielding weapons in their raised right hands and cloaks wound round their half-raised left arms. The cloaks functioned as primitive shields. In some images the cloak is would round once or twice and the two ends hang loosely down, just like the two folds of the cloak suggested by the resistivity survey and in others it is wound round more tightly to make a ball of padding. In Iron Age Europe generally, this type of cloak shield was standard equipment for non-professional soldiers.

The Cerne Giant is minimally armed, equipped as an ordinary man. A god he may be, but the people who drew him saw him battling against their enemies on the same footing as the poorest of them, a god to inspire the most disadvantaged in the community to fight on bravely.

A low knoll below the left hand may have been part of the design. A close contour survey of the knoll revealed its detailed form, and it is possible to see in its surface the features, admittedly much subdued by weathering, of a human head. It looks, from this evidence, as if the Giant was swinging a severed human head from his left hand.

The cult of the severed head is one of the best documented Iron Age cults. Head hunting was an integral part of warfare. Diodorus says of it:

'They cut off the heads of enemies killed in battle and attach them to the necks of their horses . . . They carry [the spoils] off as booty, while striking up a paean and singing a song of victory; and they nail up these first fruits on their houses. They embalm the heads of the most distinguished enemies in cedar oil and preserve them carefully in a chest, and display them with pride to strangers.'

The severed head the Cerne Giant appears to be brandishing may be the head of an important enemy, and he must therefore be returning home from battle. This is the sort of service an Iron Age British tribe would expect of its protector god. Some have ridiculed this idea, arguing that a warrior

St Augustine's Well. The wishing stone is on the left.

armed with a club could not decapitate his enemy. But they have forgotten
the belt, which shows that he was thought of as owning a knife. The knife
may have been used for finishing off a wounded enemy and then decapitat-
ing him, if the opportunity presented itself, after the battle was over.

There was often an association between severed heads and unfailing
sacred springs, and this gives a clue to a connection between the Cerne
Giant and the spring to the south known as St Augustine's Well. This has
not been excavated but it was certainly revered in the Middle Ages as a
holy well, said to be miraculously created by the tip of St Augustine's staff
in AD600 after the citizens of Cerne gave up worshipping idols, and may
have been the focus of worship in the pre-Christian era. This is suggested
by the triple-magic of the spring's properties. The rule of three is itself a
Celtic feature. First, it was a wishing well, with girls drinking at the spring
and placing a hand on the wishing stone and praying to St Catherine for a
husband. Second, it was a healing well – not only good for healing sore
eyes and general ill health but it was considered beneficial to dip new-born
babies into it at the moment when the sun's rays first touched its surface.
Third, it was prophetic. Those looking into the water at first light on Easter
morning saw the faces of all those who would die within the year.

The extensive earthworks immediately up the slope from the spring have been assumed to be connected with the abbey that occupied the site from the ninth to the sixteenth centuries, but Roman coins found in the upcast from rabbit burrows in the banks indicate that they are older. In plan, they have the general form of the Iron Age settlements on the surrounding hilltops, but they are preserved in higher relief because, conserved within the abbey precincts, they escaped being ploughed over. An Iron Age settlement here might have functioned as a host or caretaker settlement for the spring for it was common for sacred springs to become pilgrimage centres and spas, the most successful by far of these being the Iron Age Sulis sanctuary which became the centre of Roman Bath.

The Trendle, the rectangular earthwork on the hilltop above the Giant, is far too small and too weakly embanked ever to have been defensive. It is likely to have been a ritual enclosure with a wooden temple inside. Preliminary investigations are inconclusive, but may indicate signs of the post holes of an oblong temple 10 metres by 8 metres. The earthworks may have been surmounted by light fences. What deity was worshipped in this

The Cerne Giant in the 1930s with the Trendle above it.

temple? It is safe to assume that it was the same god whose image was drawn as an advertisement and waymark on the steep slope below.

Further north are the remains of a typical Iron Age farmstead, the Giant Hill farmstead. Several of the hilltops round here bear remains of Iron Age farms. One of them is directly opposite the Giant, on the crest of Weam Common Hill, and this must have been the intended viewing point for the hill figure as, from this raised position, it appears far less distorted than it does from the valley floor. The secular site of the Giant Hill settlement is separated from the ceremonial sites by a bank which runs across the crest of the ridge about halfway between the farm and the Trendle, with a token defensive ditch on its northern side; in other words, it was there to stop people, or bad spirits, getting into the precinct. Cross-ridge barriers like this were occasionally used in the Bronze and Iron Ages to mark off spur-ends or sections of ridges, to demarcate them as religious precincts and to make them special.

This all points to Cerne Abbas being an important religious cult centre in the Iron Age, with a sanctuary dedicated to the worship of the tribal protector-god, and including a sacred spring, a complex of sanctuary buildings, a small hilltop temple within an embanked enclosure, and a gigantic drawing of the god himself.

The location of Cerne Abbas is significant. In the Middle Iron Age, the territories of the Durotrigian confederation more or less coincided with the area of modern Dorset. Three large hilltowns, South Cadbury, Hod Hill and Maiden Castle, dominated Dorset and the frontiers of their three tribal lands must have run together not far from Cerne Abbas. Probably the east-west boundary ran along the major scarp three kilometres north of the Giant, exploiting a conspicuous natural barrier. The fact that major north-south and east-west routes crossed at the head of the Cerne valley makes it even more likely that this was a meeting place for representatives of the three tribal groups. In Iron Age Gaul, it was common for major religious sanctuaries to be located on frontiers in this way.

The existence of a major pre-Christian religious cult at Cerne Abbas explains the story, often dismissed as entirely fictitious, of St Augustine's visit to Cerne to put a stop to idolatry. The earliest surviving version we have of this story dates from 1091, when a Canterbury monk, Gotselin, collected it. It refers to 'the figure of Helia'. Other, later versions which may have been derived from the original Gotselin used, refer to the pagan god as Helith or Helis. In the thirteenth century, Walter of Coventry wrote, 'In that village [Cerne in the County of Dorset] the god Helith dwelt.'

When William Stukeley visited Cerne Abbas, probably in the summer of 1763, he asked the local people about the Giant. They told him exactly what it was, but they were uneducated country folk and he did not take them seriously, instead delivering to the Society of Antiquaries an incredible rigmarole of his own devising, naming the Giant Hercules Heliocus and claiming he was cut in honour of Eli, father of Caswallawn. The Fellows of the Society apparently accepted this rubbish without demur. 'The inhabitants thereabouts pretend to know nothing more of it than a traditionary account among them of its being a deity of the ancient Britons,' Stukeley laughed up his sleeve, but the thrust of the evidence would suggest that they were right. When Dr Richard Pococke visited Cerne in 1754, the villagers had evidently told him the same story. 'On the west side of the hills north of the village,' he wrote, 'is a figure cut in lines. It is called the Giant and Hele.'

'Helia' in 1081, 'Hele' in 1754, 'Helis' or 'Helith' in the twelfth and thirteenth centuries. The tradition of the Giant's name as something close to Helia, Hele, Helith or Helis was therefore perpetuated through at least 700 years. If the Cerne Giant's name in the pre-Saxon period was Helis, it must be a name in the Brittonic language, the ancestral Welsh-Cornish tongue. 'Hela' means 'to hunt' in modern Welsh: 'heliwr' means 'huntsman'. 'Hellys', which is closer still to 'Helis', means 'hunted' in Middle Cornish. 'Helis' may well have meant 'The Huntsman', which is apt for the figure on the hill. The fact that a name with no intrinsic meaning for them was conserved by an Anglo-Saxon community suggests that a genuinely ancient tradition was being honoured and kept alive at Cerne Abbas.

The future may hold further surprises. If the outline trenches are deep enough, it may be that some ancient silts have survived in them and an OSL date may be extracted. Discussions are under way to extend the research in this direction. As new archaeological techniques emerge, new possibilities for gathering data present themselves. It may be possible, within the decade, to settle the lively controversy surrounding the Cerne Giant's origins.

10

The Long Man of Wilmington

The Long Man's story is similar to that of the Cerne Giant. There are those who believe the Long Man is a modern work, on the grounds that no early documents mention him. Marples, writing in the 1940s, gave the earliest mention as 1779, which implies that the figure could be a Georgian folly made as late as the 1770s. But Marples himself commented, rightly, that it is impossible to infer the age of the figure from this date.

The discovery of the drawing of the Long Man by Sir William Burrell dated about 1766 pushed the latest possible date for the Long Man back a decade. A recent discovery of a drawing dating from 1710 pushed it back another seventy years, and that, for the moment, is the earliest recorded date. It is possible, however, that the Long Man originated in prehistory.

LOCATION.

Take the Wilmington turning south off the A27 road between Eastbourne and Lewes. The Long Man is signed on the A27. At the southern end of the village there is a car park on the right, in the shell of the ruined tithe barn, and from there the Long Man is clearly visible. A footpath leads to the foot of the giant, but it is inadvisable to climb on the figure itself. The slope is steep, the figure has suffered badly from erosion, and the view is in any case better from a distance.

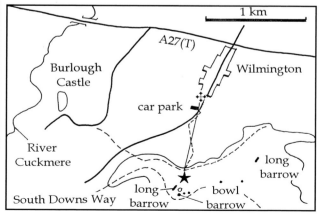

The terracettes on the Long Man show up clearly when the sun is low in the sky.

Of British giants, the Long Man of Wilmington is the most gigantic. The Cerne Giant is 55 metres from head to toe and the limited space available at Plymouth would not have allowed the lost Gogmagog to have been anywhere near as tall as that. The Long Man measures 70 metres from the tips of his toes to the crown of his head. He is standing, facing out of the hillside with his legs spread the width of his shoulders apart. His arms are half extended on each side and his hands, raised to shoulder height, are holding what appear to be lances, spears or staves.

The design is almost symmetrical, with the two vertical staves forming two sides of an unfinished rectangular frame. The illusion of a frame has been reinforced by the addition of protective fences round the figure, which have intensified visitor and livestock erosion along them. The simplicity of the image before the fences were added can be appreciated from the earliest known photograph of the Giant, taken in 1874. The only significant departure from symmetry is in the legs, which are both turned to the

Giant's right or east. This shows the giant half turning, about to walk east. The general aspect of the figure is one of great and powerful repose, as hieratic as an Egyptian pharaoh.

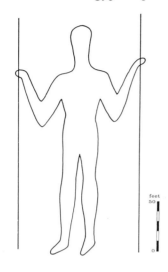

The Long Man as he is today, marked out in concrete blocks.

The figure exists in outline only. There are no tell-tale details of dress or ornament that could help identify him. He is naked, featureless, enigmatic. The pear-shaped head has no face, and it is partly this blankness that makes him a powerful archetype. It is left to the onlooker's imagination to supply the attributes, to make him a hero, a king, a god, or even – for some – a goddess. He can be whatever the observer wants him to be. All he shows are the 72 metre long staves and even they are hard to interpret. Are they ceremonial tools or weapons like Thor's hammer, the Minoan goddess's double-axe, or the Bronze Age Wessex chieftain's stone-headed mace, displaying rank and status? Do they recall an ancient survey that required ranging rods? Are they instead the leading edges of two great doors? Whatever they are, the staves offer the best opportunity of identifying this mysterious figure.

The Long Man was laid out with care, but the symmetry is not perfect. The distance between the head and the right stave is 15.5 metres, that between the head and the left stave is 14.2 metres. The staves appear to be parallel, but they are 35.5 metres apart at the top and 35 metres apart at the foot of the figure. If they were projected northwards, the staves would cross four kilometres away, 400 metres south east of Arlington church with which the Long Man has a folklore connection.

A curious feature of the drawing is the elongation that gives it its name. It has been deliberately drawn long and thin so that, although it rests on a 28 degree slope, it can be read easily from the low ground to the north. Given the heel-to-crown height of 70 metres, shoulder width of 12 metres and hip width of 8.5 metres, the Long Man has been drawn 1.9 times the height of a well proportioned man on the same lateral scale. If the elongation can be

74

corrected in this way, it should be possible to calculate the viewpoint from which it was intended the figure should be viewed. In fact, the proportions only appear correct from the air, about four degrees up from a horizontal projected northwards from the figure. There is no vantage point on terra firma along that line in the surrounding countryside so I can only conclude that the proportions were not calculated exactly and a certain degree of disproportion was accepted. The Long Man was always seen, at least from in front and by earthbound people, as a broad stocky figure with, to all appearances, the build of a short man.

There was a recent claim that the Long Man must be modern because it displays a knowledge of perspective, the stretching of the drawing being seen as an optical illusion designed to counteract the effect of foreshortening. Since perspective was a Renaissance invention, the argument ran, the Long Man must be a post-Renaissance creation. Art historians define perspective as the use of two techniques for representing three-dimensional objects on a flat surface. The first is the use of at least one-point linear perspective constructed round a vanishing point. The second is the use of aerial perspective, the gradual decrease in intensity of both tonal contrasts and intensity of colour hues as distance increases. The second does not apply as the Long Man is not a painting. The first does not apply either because there is no attempt in the drawing to create an illusion of a third dimension. Even if linear perspective had been employed, it would prove nothing about date. Overlapping forms and foreshortening to create an illusion of space can be seen on Greek carved friezes made as far back as 530 BC.

The stretching of the Long Man shows a consideration of foreshortening and a practical desire to overcome it. It is a curiosity, in that the other two surviving large ancient hill figures, the Uffington White Horse and the Cerne Giant, are not given this compensating elongation. The Cerne Giant is on a slope of comparable steepness on the east side of the Cerne valley. Opposite, there is a similar slope rising to Weam Common Hill, where an Iron Age farmstead once stood. The Cerne Giant was evidently designed to be viewed from the Weam Common Hill farmstead. It looks foreshortened and stumpy when viewed from there, but is still just 'legible'.

The Uffington Horse was drawn on an escarpment with no facing hill. It looks onto the open space of the Vale of the White Horse, from which the Horse looks like a white slash. Maybe it did not matter in the early Iron

Age that it looked little like an earthly horse – no doubt everyone then living in the area knew it was meant to be a horse, and that was enough. The Long Man was similarly placed on a north facing chalk scarp, without a facing hill that could have made a natural viewing point. Its makers can only have intended it to be viewed from the lower ground. Evidently it did matter to them that the figure should be read as a human form rather than a piece of chalk calligraphy.

The viewpoint for the Long Man has been given little consideration to date, and that may be because the initial sightline has been interrupted. The figure can no longer be seen as originally intended. Since it lies at the back of a shallow coombe it is quite difficult to see from the west and even more difficult to see from the east because of projecting spurs. It is only possible to see it clearly from the north, and it can be assumed that it was intended to be seen from a point on a line passing a few degrees east of north. A shallow spur projects from the foot slope of the chalk escarpment in this direction, and at the northern tip of this tongue of land is Wilmington churchyard.

Clearly, the churchyard is the place from which people were intended to admire or worship the Long Man. The great yew tree that still stands there was planted in AD 400, according to the most recent estimate by Allan Meredith, a clear 200 years before Christianity came to Saxon Sussex. The yew was therefore a pagan religious focus of some kind and it seems probable that the churchyard itself was some kind of sacred precinct before it acquired its present use. The sightline from the yew to the Long Man was obstructed by the building of the church, and it is likely that this positioning was quite deliberate.

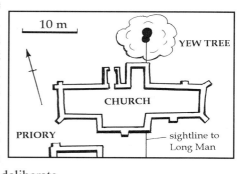

Similar things are seen at other pagan holy places. At Stanton Drew in Somerset, the church was carefully placed amid the complex of megaliths, guarding the Cove like a warder and separating it from the Great Circle. At Rudston in the Yorkshire Wolds the church was again built in the centre of major pre-Christian ceremonial landscape, right next to the Rudston Monolith. At Knowlton in Dorset, the church was built in the middle of

The ancient yew in Wilmington churchyard. The stone is of unknown antiquity.

one of the henges. At Cerne Abbas, the abbey founded by St Augustine's followers was built directly beside the Celtic sacred spring, separating it from the Cerne Giant and the Trendle.

Christian missionaries of the sixth and seventh centuries acted on specific instructions. St Augustine encountered pagan idol-worshippers in southern England and sought advice from Pope Gregory. Guidance came in the form of a long letter, which has survived. Gregory advised Augustine not to destroy pagan idols or temple, but to try to adopt them. By occupying the sites they could gradually convert the devotees of heathen cults, who would out of custom continue to honour their old holy places. The placing of Wilmington church and priory immediately to the south of the yew tree, blocking the sightline between it and the Long Man, can be seen as yet another positive response to Pope Gregory's instructions.

The Long Man would have been slightly foreshortened even seen from the churchyard. It would be necessary to float 65 metres above the ground to see the figure correctly proportioned. Perhaps it is not going too far to suggest that that possibility existed in the imagination of the Long Man's creators – that they imagined some supernatural being 65m up, viewing its own portrait from the firmament. Certainly the best view of the Long Man is to be had from the air. He is an excellent navigation aid, and in consequence had to be painted green during the Second World War to stop German bombers using him to find their way to and from London.

The lack of detail on the figure, and the shortage of archaeological evidence, leads some people to hope for a revelation through folklore. This line of inquiry is fairly fruitless. There is an oft-repeated story of two giants, one living on Firle Beacon, one on Windover Hill, the next big hill to the east. They quarrelled, as giants do, lobbed stones at each other and the Windover giant was felled. This has been taken by some to indicate that a second figure may once have graced the northern slope of Firle Beacon, which would indeed make a fine hill figure site.

In 1963, Tom Lethbridge wrote in a letter:

'The tradition of two figures at Wilmington is remarkable. I was at school at Rottingdean 50 years ago or so and some old fellow who taught us carpentry and was known as Offa told us there were two giants up in the hills to the eastward and they were Adam and Eve. Of course I didn't pay much attention . . . but it stuck in my memory.'

He also referred disparagingly to 'a woman Simpson'. Jacqueline Simpson had also got hold of the two giants tradition. In the mid-nineteenth century there was a local story that the second figure was on Hindover Hill, a steep hill two kilometres south west of Windover. It does seem possible that there was a second figure at or near Wilmington, although whether it was at Hindover or elsewhere is a matter of guesswork. The Hindover site was chosen for the Litlington Horse, and maybe that was what attracted the idea of an earlier figure to pair with the Long Man. Maybe it was the pairing of the names – Windover, Hindover – that generated the idea of two figures. The Reverend T Bunston, lecturing in 1912, repeated a story he had heard about the Long Man chasing a woman and falling over on his back. Possibly 'the woman' and 'Eve' are faint but genuine recollections of a lost female figure in the Sussex Downs.

Folklore is hard to evaluate, and useless without corroboration. No photographic or archaeological evidence has yet been offered in support of a second hill figure east of Lewes.

Another story, collected by the Reverend W D Parish in 1873, asserts that there is a cock on the hillside immediately to the east of the Long Man. A resident of Wilmington, James Levett, claimed he 'saw the rooster very plain', but it was an image that came and went with the changing light. The existence of a cock beside the Giant was taken to signify that the giant was really St Peter, whose betrayals were marked by the crowing cock. The fact that Wilmington church was dedicated to St Peter seemed to lend the story weight. There is, however, no evidence that there was ever a second image of any kind beside the Long Man.

Traces of wall paintings have been found in Wilmington church. In black letter were the words:

> 'I had rather been a doorkeeper in the house of my God, than to dwell in the tents of ungodliness.'

The Long Man appears to be standing in a doorway, so perhaps the villagers at one time saw him as the doorkeeper in the house of the Lord.

Traces of Long Man folklore survive at Arlington. It is said that once an avenue led all the way from village churchyard to the feet of the Long Man, and the Wilmington churchyard yew is one of the surviving trees of this avenue. There is certainly a footpath across the fields from Arlington to Wilmington, but no clear evidence of an avenue. Arlington churchyard is, however, an ancient settlement site. When the church was restored in the nineteenth century, Roman tiles and pottery were discovered beneath the nave floor. The implications of this bit of folklore are that the Roman or Romano-British community living at Arlington walked along a tree-lined road to the Long Man and that Arlington was the home of the giant's creators.

The Long Man's origins and identity have been discussed frequently, and I doubt whether any of the theories so far proposed will prove to match the truth. Candidates for the Long Man include Beowulf, a Saxon warrior or hay-maker, Wotan, Baldur, a Roman emperor, the mysterious Dodman who surveyed ley lines with his ranging rods, the Fighting Man badge of King Harold, Herne the Hunter and Samson about to pull down on himself the two middle pillars upon which the house stood.

In my 1983 book, *The Wilmington Giant*, I reviewed many of the theories and found them all unsatisfactory for one reason or another. I came down in favour of a neolithic origin, partly because of the Long Man's monumentality – compare the ambitious deployment of giant stones at Stonehenge and Avebury – and partly because of the high concentration of neolithic sites at the eastern end of the South Downs. In the fairly small area east of Lewes, for example, there are as many as nine long barrows and long barrow sites, whereas there are only two between Lewes and the longitude of Chichester. This empty stretch separates the Windover territory, if it can be called that, from the chalk plains of Wessex, which have a high density of long barrows. The tracks at the foot and on the crest of the scarp are believed to have been in use as neolithic trade routes. There is a causewayed enclosure just 3 km to the east, on Combe Hill, and neolithic flint mines cluster immediately above the Long Man on both east and west sides.

It also looked as if the iconography would fit within a neolithic context. There is evidence from a range of neolithic ritual sites in Britain that earthen, stone and timber circles and near circles frequently had their entrances oriented on solstice sunrise and sunset positions, the most famous being the midsummer sunrise orientation of Stonehenge. The idea of a sun god arriving on midsummer morning, flying in along the Stonehenge Avenue to enter the magic circle between the portal formed by the Heel Stone and its missing partner, led me to interpret the Long Man's staves as the ceremonial portals, whether in stone or timber, of some lost Sussex version of Stonehenge.

The Long Man was not holding staves, nor opening a pair of doors, but holding his hands out in a hieratic gesture as he flew in between the portals to preside over the high summer crop-ripening. The hill figure was a picture of a mythic seasonal event, with the Long Man as the divine herald of the harvest.

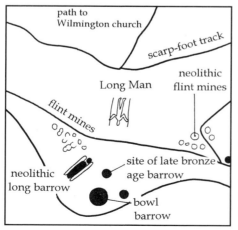

Prehistoric remains cluster round the Long Man.

That my neolithic hypothesis is as vulnerable as several of the alternative hypotheses is now obvious. When I offered it, no henges were known in the south east. Although some henge-like enclosures have subsequently been discovered, for instance during the construction of the Brighton bypass, there is still no identifiable local monument to which the staves might be a reference. However, the doors of possibility are still open and the fact that major prehistoric sites are still being discovered in Sussex is a cause for optimism.

Windover Hill was a site of both economic and ceremonial activity in the neolithic period and the two types of activity were probably not separated. Stone for axes and maces was prized, not just for its practical use but for where it came from – it gained a special value if it came from a special place.

Windover continued to hold its position as a ceremonial centre of some kind in the Bronze Age and possibly in the Iron Age too. It is known, from other prehistoric ceremonial centres, that they tended to be long lasting, with adaptations and re-interpretations crossing cultural boundaries. The Uffington Horse was well maintained over a period of 3,000 years, with both the Horse and the features round it undergoing periodic rehabilitation and redefinition by new generations of people.

The neolithic long barrow in front of the Horse was re-used for Roman burials; the Bronze Age barrow between the two was re-used for Saxon burials; the Iron Age hill fort became the site of a late Roman fair, to say nothing of the much later fairs associated with eighteenth and nineteenth century scourings.

The flurry of neolithic activity on and round Windover Hill, which is represented by the two long barrows, the trackways, the flint mines, and a possible settlement at Burlough Castle, evidently continued into the Bronze Age, with the major aristocratic bowl barrow burial right on the summit, probably built in the early Bronze Age. An unusual red-enamelled bronze ornament, now in Birmingham Museum and misleadingly known as the Arlington Terret, was found during the excavation of the chalk quarry between the Giant's head and the bowl barrow. The quarry was known in the nineteenth century as Longman's Pit. The bronze ornament was probably made in the late Bronze Age and comes from a barrow burial on the site of the quarry, which therefore marks the site of another princely grave. A bronze hoard was buried below the figure, down at Wilmington Green.

A typical 'Celtic' carved stone head found in Wilmington village shows the area continuing as a religious site of some kind into the Iron Age. The planting of a yew on the churchyard site in AD 400 again suggests that Wilmington was a focus of pagan religious activity – and the churchyard represents, as has been stated, the best vantage point for viewing the Long

Sir William Burrell's 1766 drawing.

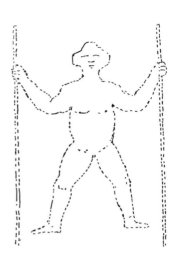

The Rowley drawing of 1710.

The recently discovered Pownall drawing.

Man. If Windover Hill was an economic, social, political or religious centre – and possibly a shifting blend of these functions from 3000 BC until the arrival of Christian missionaries between 600 and 650 – the hill figure could have been created at any time during that period. It need not, as I once thought, have been the first component in the sequence. It may have been among the last – a summative statement.

The Long Man's outline is blank and there has been a great deal of speculation that significant detail that may have helped to identify him has been lost. Petrie thought he could see traces of facial features, but if he did there is no proof that they were of any antiquity.

Sir William Burrell's drawing of 1766 shows eyes, nose, mouth and hair, and the Rowley drawing of 1710, shows eyes, nose, mouth and a hat. However, later drawings, such as the nineteenth century sketches of Pownall, Plenderleath and Phene, make it plain that no facial features survived. Was the Long Man clothed or naked? Burrell drew in the V of an open-necked shirt and, although this is believed to be an invention, Pownall

82

drew in the same feature. Whether this is to suggest that the Long Man was always intended, from the beginning, to be fully clothed is open to speculation, but it may be that nudity as such was never intended to be part of the statement. It should not be assumed that the Long Man was at some early stage equipped with a phallus like the Cerne Giant.

A major problem in dealing with the Long Man is that it is not the original image at all. Today it is an assemblage of white-painted concrete blocks half-buried in the soil, which proves a disappointment to the many visitors who take the trouble to walk up to the figure There is a second hill figure in the South Downs – a buried Giant – and it is a disturbing thought that he does not lie precisely beneath the concrete markers.

The site was handed over by the Duke of Devonshire to the Sussex Archaeological Trust for restoration and maintenance in 1874. The Reverend de St Croix and a team of helpers marked out the figure, which had grassed over and all but disappeared, with yellow bricks. Fragments of yellow brick can still be found on the site. The vicar was, in effect, rescuing the monument from extinction.

For as long as anyone could remember the Long Man of Wilmington had been a Green Giant, which means that there can have been no scouring in the nineteenth century. Some have suggested that this is how the Long Man was intended to look from the beginning, but it seems more likely that the faint depressions visible in 1874 were all that remained of silted up and grassed over trenches cut through the soil and down to the frost-shattered chalk beneath. As at Uffington, it was probably found during the initial cutting that the discoloured and weathered chalk exposed in the trench floors gave a poor image, and chalk rubble was added from elsewhere. A similar technique was used at Cerne. There is archaeological evidence for this.

At the time of the re-bricking in the 1960s, Eric Holden took the opportunity to open some sample trenches. It is odd, given the tiny amount of excavated evidence available, that the implications of his sections have not been fully explored. Under the right, or east, shin there was only 30cm of soil before the undisturbed chalk surface was reached. Disappointingly, there was no sign of a deep trench excavated into the bedrock, but there was a broad shallow depression 7cm deep. A similar shallow and ill-defined depression was found on the bedrock surface under the line marking the top of the head. Under the right stave, the depression in the natural chalk surface was about 60cm wide and again a few centimetres deep – negligible enough for some to say that no trace of an outline trench survives, and that therefore there was no outline trench.

But how did the shallow depressions get there? Turf and soil seem to have been removed from a trench 80cm wide at the top and tapering in towards a chalk floor 30–60cm below the soil surface level. Initially, and during the run-up to scourings, or rather rebuildings, the trench floor was exposed to the weather and suffered denudation from frost, livestock trampling and rainwash.

The trench Holden made through the Long Man's east stave revealed a section through an ancient trench that was u-shaped and appears to have been lined with chalk rubble. The old trench is no longer filled with rubble, possibly because it was left open and unrepaired for a long time, became eroded by rain and livestock, was allowed to grass over and gradually filled with soil.

The drawing made by Phene shortly before the bricking.

Phene in 1872 thought the outline trenches were backfilled in the Middle Ages in a deliberate act of decommissioning, but the process could have happened simply through neglect and subsequent reclamation by nature.

The ghost of the ancient trench shows that the outline would have been around 80cm wide. It was far bolder as a drawing, far more conspicuous in the landscape, than the present too finely drawn figure. The silting and grassing over phase may have lasted more than 200 years. The outline had virtually vanished by 1874, and the way Rowley drew it with a dotted line shows that it was an ill-defined grass figure in 1710.

Mrs Ann Downs lived at Wilmington Priory, directly below the Giant, in the 1850s. From there she was able to watch the Giant's outline disappearing and reappearing with the changing light. In 1873, Parish noted that when John Guy, then aged 82, was a boy the Giant was sometimes known as 'The Green Man'. That would have been around 1800. Unfortunately the first accurate survey of the Giant was not done until after the 1874 bricking, and so far no photograph of the hillside before 1874 has been identified, so there are some difficulties in reconstructing what the pre-1874 figure looked like.

The 1874 photograph, taken immediately after the bricking, proves that at least some bricks were misplaced. A print of this photo was passed down through the de St Croix family and, in 1969, Holden managed to borrow it and have it re-photographed for an article about the Long Man. The quality of reproduction was poor. I tracked down the high-quality glass negative and had the area showing the hill figure enlarged. The crisp white outline of the new left, or west, leg overlaps a faint dark image in the turf, made by a shallow depression and possibly deeper soil, marking the earlier position of the leg. Almost the entire leg was incorrectly bricked. It was originally turned outwards, slightly more splayed, with the foot pointing outwards and diagonally down the slope.

When Holden dug his 1969 trenches, he found twelve small pieces of Roman or Romano-British pottery about halfway down through the fill. Little has been made of this find, but I have subsequently found another nine fragments of the same fabric, eroded by sheep out of the soil at the midriff. Although the total volume is small, the colour and texture variations show that they are fragments of several different pots or tiles. Two with flat surfaces, one of mine, one of Holden's, must have come from tiles. One of the nearest Roman buildings to the Long Man was at Arlington, which perhaps suggests there may after all be truth in the folklore.

Halfway down through the fill Holden also found a single piece of sandstone, presumably local greensand from Wilmington village. These finds indicate that material was brought up onto the site and deposited in the outline trenches, in exactly the way one would expect. The fact that the Roman tile fragments have mostly weathered edges suggests that they were collected from the settlement some time after it had fallen in ruins. The fragments may therefore represent a repair to the Long Man late during the Roman occupation. Why non-white, and therefore on the face of it unsuitable, material should have been brought from so far afield when there was plenty of chalk available near at hand remains a mystery. If substantial quantities of orange-red tile were added to the white fill, the intention may have been to create a Pink Giant, but the presence of the greensand fragment suggests that the process was more random than that.

The foreshortened Long Man regenerated from the 1874 photographs.

There was an awareness even at the time of the bricking that a mistake had been made, and Bunston said in his 1912 lecture that the feet had 'pointed downwards in the line of the form', by which he meant that they continued the diagonal line of the legs. His remark implies that the right leg was also bricked incorrectly, at least as far as the angle of the foot is concerned. Careful study of the enhanced enlargement of the 1874 photograph shows that the original right leg was slightly further out and the fork of the legs about half a metre further up the slope. It also shows that the original right foot did indeed point diagonally downwards. It may be possible to extract more detail from the 1874 photo by computer.

The extensive geophysical surveys I undertook in 1997–98 are still being processed. They, too, promise to reveal further details about the shape of the Long Man as he was before 1874. The adjustments established so far have already to an extent renewed the Giant and made him into a significantly different figure. He has become more lithe, energetic, dynamic, distinctly more elfin. Instead of standing majestically like a pharaoh, he seems, as some nineteenth century observers commented, to be stepping down the hill, or flying out of the hillside, springing out like Puck or Ariel.

No doubt even this newly discovered giant will suggest different associations to different observers and engender renewed debate.

11

The Wandlebury Giant

We do not know what the figure looked like, and depend entirely on a few brief documented references, dating as far back as the sixteenth century. The gigantic figure of a god called Gogmagog was evidently visible at that time. The Gogmagog Hills take their name from the figure, and the first known mention of the place name is 1576. The first mention of the Wandlebury Giant itself came in 1605 in a book by Bishop Joseph Hall:

> 'A Giant called All Paunch, who was of incredible Height of body, not like him whose Picture the Schollers of Cambridge go to see at Hogmagog Hills, but rather like him that ought the two Apple Teeth which were digged out of a well in Cambridge, that were little less than a man's head [in size].'

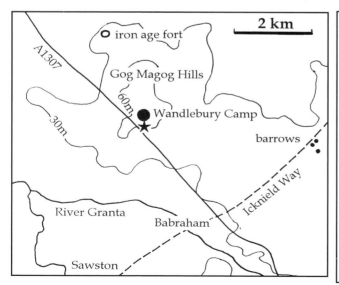

LOCATION

The Gogmagog Hills lie to the south of Cambridge. Access to Wandlebury Camp, an Iron Age hillfort, is from the A1397. The controversial hill figure is no longer visible, and there is disagreement as to whether it was inside the earthworks or on the south-facing slope immediately outside.

The idea that giants' teeth might be found was apparently widely held. It was said that when the foundations of the Citadel were being dug at Plymouth at the end of the seventeenth century the gigantic molars of the giant Gogmagog were discovered.

The origin of the name Gogmagog is disputed. It could have been borrowed from the name of Biblical giants, or it could derive from a Brittonic name, or, more likely still, it could have begun as a Brittonic name that has evolved towards the Biblical name. It has been pointed out that the form of the word is similar to an old Cambridge word for 'snail' – hodmedod – and it may be that the name Hodmedod, later turning into Gogmagog, was first applied to the earthworks of Wandlebury Camp, the plan of which may have been seen in the Middle Ages as similar to the spiral pattern on a snail shell. In the seventeenth century there is a form halfway in between – Hogmagog. So the Giant's name may have started off as a name for the place, rather than of a deity. The name Wandlebury probably derives from Waendel's burh, the fort of the Anglo-Saxon hero.

The fort was used before and during the Roman occupation as a frontier fort by the Iceni tribe. In the eighteenth century, the camp was included in a landscaped garden project by Lord Godolphin. The inner of the two banks was levelled and pushed into the ditch, and the outer bank was broken through in several places. If the figure was cut in the turf inside the earthwork, as asserted by John Layer in 1640, it seems almost certain that it was destroyed by this improving activity. Layer describes the Giant as cut between the trench of Wandlebury Camp. He cannot have meant 'between the two trenches', as this would have made the figure hopelessly small. He clearly meant 'within the bounding trench' or 'inside the Camp'.

Layer says that the Wandlebury Giant was a human form, and seems to be emphasising that it was not as big as the 'All-Paunch' he referred to. He says explicitly that the hill figure was:

'a high and mighty portraiture of a giant wch the Schollars of Cambridge cut upon the turf or superficies of the earth within the said trench, and not unlikely called it Gogmagog, which I have seen is but late discontinued'.

Whether Layer had good reason for supposing the students had cut the figure is not known, although it is likely that students volunteered to scour an ancient figure. There is documentary evidence that undergraduates from Oxford cleaned one or both of the Chiltern crosses, so it is quite possible that Cambridge undergaduates did the same for the Wandlebury Giant. There is a further clue in Layer's odd comment that something was 'but late discontinued'. How could a hill figure be 'discontinued'? It seems far more likely that he was thinking of the scouring or cleaning that every hill figure needs to keep it alive and that could certainly be discontinued, so it may be that when he wrote of it in 1640 there had been no recent scourings.

Tom Lethbridge did not accept that the Giant had been destroyed, nor that it had been inside the Camp. In 1954 he apparently made up his mind to rediscover the lost Giant, which he believed had lain just outside the earthworks. He had been told by a Cambridge museum assistant, Sammy Cowles, that as a child Sammy had spoken to old man who in turn remembered in his own childhood seeing the Wandlebury Giant from Sawston. To Lethbridge this amounted to proof that the Giant was not cut on a horizontal surface, was not sheltered behind Iron Age banks, and must have been on the Sawston-facing slope outside the Camp.

Having decided where the Giant had once existed, Lethbridge hammered an iron bar through the soil to determine its depth. In this way he was able to map the pattern of depressions in the chalk bedrock surface. The result was a peculiar-looking image, which Lethbridge sketched and sent to Sir Thomas Kendrick at the British Museum. Kendrick replied incautiously (and by telegram):

'Rear quarter of an animal. Walking (not galloping) white horse, May the Lord be with you'.

Encouraged, Lethbridge went on with his soundings, adding another figure, which he again sketched and sent off. This time it was Cyril Fox who replied, again showing insufficient caution:

'. . . female with two horses, probably Epona. Congratulations.'

Then he found a chariot and a huge sword-waving warrior with a round shield, completing a frieze 90m long and 36m high. He excavated the central figure, the goddess, and told the *The Times* about his discovery of a hitherto lost 3,000 year old hill figure.

His book, *Gogmagog,* is a delight to read, but the research method he used is unlikely to have been an appropriate one for finding a lost hill figure. Sceptics at the time it was published in 1956 believed that the irregularities in the bedrock surface were better explained by patterns of

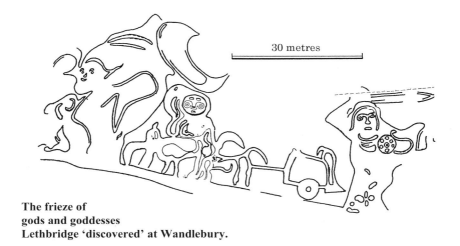

The frieze of
gods and goddesses
Lethbridge 'discovered' at Wandlebury.

periglacial weathering in the last cold stage of the Ice Age. More recent excavations on slopes well away from Lethbridge's frieze have led archaeologists and geomorphologists alike to the same conclusion. It also seems that Lethbridge put too much reliance on a third-hand account of a nineteenth century sighting of the figure. Although he expresses it oddly, Layer says that the figure was within the bank, and Dr Dale, an antiquarian who saw the Camp between 1722 and 1738, told the same story – the Giant was 'cut in the turf in the middle of the camp.'

If Lethbridge was probing and excavating the genuine site of the hill figure he probably did irreparable damage to it, but it is more likely that it was inside the enclosure all the time, and already destroyed long before by landscape gardening in the eighteenth century. I am wary of a researcher who identifies the central figure as a Sun God in December 1956, but a month later has added two conspicuous nipples to turn it into Epona the Celtic Horse Goddess.

Tom Lethbridge was remembered by one of his contemporaries from student days as a great joker. The friend in question visited Wandlebury while Lethbridge was working on it and commended it as Tom's 'best jape so far.' Apparently Lethbridge never spoke to him again. The truth is that Lethbridge may have led people up the garden path out of mixed motives, partly humour, partly a keen desire to cock a snook at the archaeological establishment. The Wandlebury gods became the mirror of his ego and his reputation, so he was unable to own up.

Lethbridge argued that if the figure was where Layer and Dale said it was, it could not have been an Iron Age antiquity, partly because it would have been invisible, partly because it would have got in the way of the operation of the site as a fortress.

Paul Newman, who believes the figure was within the fort, argues that this tends towards a date for the figure long after the hillfort fell out of use, and therefore opts for a medieval date. This may be right, but it is worth remembering that although all such monuments are termed hillforts, there is no reason to suppose that they had but a single use, and evidence from other excavated forts shows that some at least had a ceremonial function as well. Several, like Maiden Castle, had shrines or temples in them. Some may even have been primarily ceremonial in function. I have also seen air photograph evidence that one West Country Iron Age hillfort had a weapon-wielding warrior figure drawn on the horizontal land surface inside it, covering a substantial proportion of its area.

It would seem, from all the evidence taken together, that Wandlebury was similar and that there was a gigantic drawing of a warlike figure within the enclosure of Wandlebury Camp. It was very likely contemporary with the Iron Age use of the site, endowing it with special ceremonial, and probably religious, significance.

Wandlebury even has its own, apparently Celtic, legend. It was recounted by Gervase of Tilbury in 1211, who told of Osbert, a knight, who travelled to Cambridge and was regaled over supper with the story that if a warrior were to enter Wandlebury fort alone at dead of night and cry, 'Knight to knight, come forth!' an opponent would appear to answer his challenge. Osbert went to Wandlebury, called out the challenge and was confronted by a formidable opponent who unseated him from his horse, then inflicted a lance wound in his thigh, which at first Osbert did not notice. Osbert's wound later healed, but re-opened every year on the anniversary of the combat.

There is no evidence from the fort itself of the beliefs of its Iron Age or dark age Celtic inhabitants, but the story is insistent in its link to the place, unusually so for an ancient tale, and it has the character of an ancient Celtic tale. There are close parallels with the story of Peredur's combat with the black man who leaps out from under a slab – implying an association with a spring – dressed in rusty armour and riding a bony horse. Both fights take place on a hill, a classic Celtic *locus sanctus*. The man's huge size, his black and red colouring and the implied connection with a water source suggest a spirit of the underworld. Another version of the same story is told in Owein, where a bowl of water is ritually poured onto a special summoning slab to call up the Black Knight for battle.

It may be that the story is a genuine survival from the Iron Age, or it may equally represent a dark age, perhaps sixth century AD, Celtic reflection on the Gogmagog figure inside the fort. It would have made a deep impression on strangers who ventured in and saw the mysterious and otherworldly giant chalk figure glimmering in the moonlight.

12

Gogmagog at Plymouth

Below the Royal Citadel built in Charles II's time, there were once two
Giants. The Citadel incorporated within its walls an ancient chapel of St
Catherine, south of which was a Giant's Grot, a cave which had some
folklore association with the hill figure; the cave became the site of the
magazine. The images of the Giants were cut on hard grey limestone, and
would not have shown up as well as the chalk figures further east. It has
been suggested that they were reddened with earth to make them more visible but this is only a guess and one might as well

LOCATION.

*On a grassy south
facing slope between
the south eastern
corner of the Citadel
in Plymouth and the
road following the
shore.
It is immediately west
of the promontory
known as Fisher's
Nose, and more or less
marks the entrance to
Sutton Harbour.
The ancient image,
which once looked out
across Plymouth
Sound, has vanished
without trace, but its
site is well attested.*

assume that chalk or whitewash was used, which would have been far more effective. What the Giants looked like is uncertain, apart from the fact that they wielded clubs and one was considerably bigger than the other. Some have proposed that originally there was only one Giant and the other, probably the smaller one, was added later. Unfortunately no drawings have survived to show what they looked like.

It is assumed that they were destroyed when the Citadel was extended in 1666, engineered by Sir Bernard Gomme. The slope below the wall was regraded at that time and the Giants may have been either hacked away or buried, but that is not known for certain, and it may be that the Giants still exist below the municipally tended grass.

The fullest description of the Plymouth Giants is tantalisingly brief. Richard Carew, an Elizabethan historian, wrote in 1602 that two figures were cut into the turf above the Sound.

> 'Upon the Haw at Plymouth, there is cut upon the ground the portraiture of two men, the one bigger, the one lesser, with clubbes in their hands (who they term Gogmagog) and (as I have learned) it is renewed by the order of the Townsmen, which should infer the monument of some moment.'

In 1630, Westcote referred again to the 'portraiture of two men of the largest volume, yet the one surpassing the other in every way,' and added: 'These they name to be Corineus and Gogmagog.' Perhaps because of its unique urban setting, this hill figure is unusually well documented. Entries in the Audit and Receiver's Book of the Corporation of Plymouth is evidence that the image existed well before the seventeenth century, and that it was, as Carew said, cleaned and repaired at the civic cost:

1486   Item paid to Cotewyll for ye renewing of ye picture of Gogmagog upon ye howe.
1500–1 Item paid for making clene of Gogmagog apon ye howe.
1529–30 Cleansing of Gogmagog 8d.
1541–2 Item paid to William Hawkyns, baker, for cuttyng of Gogmagog, the picture of the Gyaunt, on the hawe.
1566–7 20d new cutting of Gogmagog.

The Audit Book refers to the picture of Gogmagog as if it were a single figure – just one giant, not two. One suggestion that has been made and repeated is that the second giant was added relatively late, perhaps the 'new cutting' in 1566, and the higher cost reflects the creation of the second figure at that time. If so, it would probably have been the result of assimilating West Country folklore as popularised by Geoffrey of Monmouth's *History of the Kings of Britain*. Plymouth was seen as the place where Corineus had his wrestling match with Gogmagog. A party of Trojans led by Brutus landed at Totnes in Devon, it was said, to find that Britain was inhabited by a tribe of giants. One of the colonists, Prince Corineus, was keen to fight the giants, who obligingly attacked the Trojans at Totnes. Corineus engaged in single combat with Goemagot, the leader of the giants. Although he sustained three broken ribs in the wrestling match, Corineus succeeded in rushing Goemagot to a cliff top and hurling him over. The giant king was torn to pieces on the rocks below, at the place called Lam Goemagot. Lam Goemagot, the place of the Giant's Fall, is believed to be the present Lamhay Hill, a low hill close to the Citadel.

According to one view, Plymouth's claim to be the location for this exploit was reinforced by the creation, some time after the publication of Geoffrey's book in the twelfth century, but before 1486, of the hill figure depicting the fatal struggle.

There is another scenario that is at least equally likely. The larger figure, a single club-wielding male, was made in the Iron Age as an icon of the local protector god, fulfilling much the same function as the Cerne Giant, but for a tribe of the Dumnonii confederation rather than for a Durotrigian tribe. The site is particularly significant from this point of view, as there was an Iron Age settlement in front of the image, on Mount Batten.

The narrow peninsula of Mount Batten projects into Plymouth Sound like a thin accusing finger pointing at the Citadel. On its tip there was an Iron Age settlement that continued into the period of the Roman occupation. Archaeologically, the site is hard to unravel because of its subsequent over-use as a fort in the Civil War, a burial ground later in the seventeenth century for victims of plague and shipwreck, limestone quarrying in the eighteenth and nineteenth centuries and the creation of a naval station in 1913.

A sample pit revealed mixed finds from the sixth century BC to the twentieth century AD. The prehistoric finds that point to an Iron Age settlement included a bronze pin in *La Tene* style, apparently a French import; a swan's neck sunflower pin, imported from Scotland; a spring for a

The site of Gogmagog. The Citadel wall is to the left, Sutton harbour in the background.

brooch; and a ferrule. Among the Romano-British finds were coins of Antoninus Pius, some roof tiles and several Romano-British south western ware pots. The finds as a whole point to Mount Batten as a wealthy and important late Iron Age port, with long distance trading contacts.

It seems likely that the Gogmagog figure was the divine protector of the Mount Batten settlement, placed where it could be clearly seen across the water. It was possibly intended to protect the sailors as they made their way in and out of harbour. Gogmagog may, also like the Cerne Giant, have had a double function as a waymark. Plymouth Sound has a complicated indented coastline and it would have helped seafarers identify the route into Sutton Harbour and easily find Mount Batten. The landscape setting certainly supports an Iron Age origin.

The original purpose of the image was probably forgotten or overlaid by later reinterpretations by the Middle Ages, and the excitement of associating Plymouth with the vanquishing of Geoffrey's Goemagot probably led to the cutting of a 'Corineus' figure to turn the Iron Age god into a doomed British giant-king. In 1437, Plymouth was granted mayoral privileges by Act of Parliament, and it may have been shortly after this, in a burst of civic pride, that Corineus was cut, perhaps around 1440.

It seems unlikely that more will be learned about this intriguing site. If the explanation offered here is correct, though, it implies that turf-cut or rock-cut images like the one at Cerne Abbas were made at many other places, besides the ones already discovered.

The Shotover Giant

This is a lost hill figure. It was reported, but not drawn or described, in the seventeenth century. Its location is not known but a likely site is on one of the many slopes of this substantial hill east of Oxford. The name Shotover provides no useful clues. It derives not from *Chateau Vert,* as is sometimes said, but from *sceot ofer,* Anglo-Saxon for 'steep slope'. It is not, and never has been, a hill that was shot over by Robin Hood.

Once again, fakelore is no help. The hill is fairly steep sided and flat-topped, the plateau surface being known as 'The Plain'. The old road that crosses the Plain from east to west is a section of the original

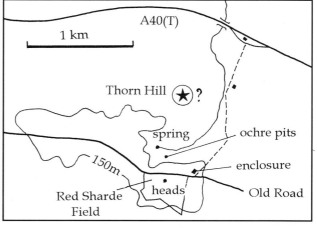

Thorn hill. Is this the site of the Shotover Giant?

London-Oxford road and was a notorious haunt of highwaymen in the eighteenth century. Now it is a quiet backwater frequented by dog-walkers, joggers and antiquarians.

The fact that in the seventeenth century it was assumed that the Shotover Giant was the work of high-spirited Oxford undergraduates suggests that the image may have been of the same provocative character as the Cerne Giant. If it is assumed that the Shotover Giant was an Iron Age icon of the same type as the Cerne Giant, it will be necessary to look around the Plain and its surrounding scarps for further similarities with Cerne Abbas. At Cerne, the hill figure was associated with a sacred spring near its foot and a sub-rectangular earthwork on higher ground, all forming components of a ceremonial complex. Is there a candidate for a sacred spring on Shotover Hill? There is, in fact, a spring in a secluded coombe associated with ochre pits that are known from documents to have been worked from the Middle Ages until the early twentieth century. In 1677, the scientist Dr Plot, in his *Natural History of Oxfordshire,* described ten kinds of earth in this neighbourhood. The fourth stratum, he said, was a white clay good for making pipes, 'models, gargils, antiches'. In fact the white clay was used some 2,000 years ago, in

The ochre pits. The spring is off the picture to the left.

the Romano-British period, for making models just as he described, at a site on the Plain close to the spring.

Fifty metres to the south of the spring were several kilns apparently for manufacturing pottery. In 1952 Mark Hassall found a mould for making heads in the same field that in 1593 was known as Red Sharde Field. It is planted with potatoes and has a bright russet ironsand soil. Among the products of this Romano-British industry were some elaborately detailed female heads with long flowing hair.

The Shotover heads.

Were these the heads of deities – water sprites, perhaps? To my eye they look rather forbidding, but tastes vary. And was the site as a whole devoted to manufacturing objects dedicated to a religious cult of some kind?

A little way off, still on the

Plain, but to the east of the spring, is a rectangular earthwork, not unlike the Trendle above the Cerne Giant though preserved in higher relief. This may or may not be an Iron Age enclosure, and its presence adjacent to the Shotover House avenue, itself a substantial earthwork, hints that it may after all be connected with the major landscaping programme of Sir James Tyrrell at the beginning of the eighteenth century.

Nevertheless, there are within a small area a rectangular earthwork, a vigorous spring and evidence of the production of cult objects in the third-fourth centuries AD. If there was a hill figure to go with this complex, it could have been cut on any of the three sides of Thorn Hill. On balance, it seems to me most likely to have been the north facing slope, as a hill figure placed there would have been visible from a much larger area, and would have helped people to find the entrance to the obscure, L-shaped coombe where the spring was hidden. In the Romano-British period, a road ran over Shotover from south to north, from Dorchester-on-Thames to Alchester, not far west of Red Sharde Field, and there were three settlements on it. The kilns were about a kilometre to the east of these.

This reconstruction is highly speculative. It is, I fear, the best I can do until further field evidence is available. The distribution of chance finds of Mesolithic, Neolithic, Bronze Age and Iron Age dates shows that people visited or occupied Shotover Hill throughout that long period, but without showing any preference for the spring area.

An engraving of 1750 shows a bird's-eye view of Shotover House and its gardens. The formal gardens, ponds and avenue are visible, but not the Giant. The evidence, incomplete as it is, suggests that an ancient hill figure, possibly of the same general type as the Cerne Giant, existed on Shotover Hill as late as the seventeenth century, but did not survive until the second half of the eighteenth century.

14

Lost Giants

This book was started with the intention of giving a summary of existing knowledge concerning the older hill figures in Britain, partly to clear the air of misconceived ideas, which abound, partly to set the monuments more firmly in their landscape settings. Because individual hill figures inspire strong local loyalties there has often been a distinct lack of uniformity in approach. Some figures have been investigated with admirable scientific and historical rigour, others have been the subject of a disproportionate amount of wild theorising; still others have had to endure unjustified and long-term neglect. I was surprised, for example, to find that I had to carry out my own survey of the Watlington Mark which, as it happened, was easy to do.

It sometimes comes about that a critical review of old data and ideas can lead on to some new ideas and the gathering of more data, and I have felt, while writing, that that has been happening.

While hill figures must not be forced into a single uniform class, some significant points in common are emerging. The current academic fashion is to see the older hill figures as 'early modern' creations of the sixteenth and seventeenth centuries. The principal argument in favour of this is the admitted lack of unambiguous documentation from earlier centuries, but the weakness of this position is obvious. There are no title deeds for Stonehenge that prove either its Mesolithic origin or its decommissioning in the Bronze Age, and no one would expect such documents ever to have been made. There are no documentary references to my family before the 1690s – as a dynasty of farm labourers it was beneath notice – but I think it is reasonable to suppose that it existed nevertheless.

It has also been argued that the Cerne Giant, to take but one example, is likely to be early modern because the other giants are also early modern. The circularity of this line of reasoning is too obvious to counter. Another, rather desperate, argument is that the giants were not at Romano-Celtic holy places but two universities and a seaport, the implication being that the giants were made as pranks by undergraduates and sailors. It is true that the Wandlebury Gogmagog was close to Cambridge and the Shotover Giant was near Oxford; the Plymouth Gogmagog is admittedly now engulfed in a major seaport; but the Long Man of Wilmington was nowhere near a college or a port. In fact, a close examination of the sites does indicate either likely or possible associations for many of the figures with Romano-British or older ritual centres.

Several of the older figures are likely to have their origin in the Iron Age, which lasted from approximately 700 BC until the Roman invasion of AD 43. The Uffington Horse is the first and only hill figure to have yielded an 'absolute' date, in the sense that a laboratory has scientifically dated material from the site, and that comes out at 1400—600 BC, and most likely towards the end of that time window. Iconography demands that the Cerne Giant belongs to the Iron Age too, although as yet there is no OSL or any other absolute date. For the Long Man of Wilmington there is neither absolute date nor iconography. It can only be dated indirectly, and therefore less reliably, by association with other monuments in the surrounding landscape, and they suggest a date between 3000 BC and AD 400.

The Red Horse of Tysoe has something of the dash and stylised grace of the Uffington White Horse and may therefore also be Iron Age. The Plymouth Gogmagog brandished a club like the Cerne Giant and faced a major Iron Age and Romano-British settlement, so it is likely itself to have been created in the Iron Age or during the Roman occupation. From the geographical associations of the Wandlebury and Shotover Giants and the cursory descriptions of them that survive, they too may belong to the Iron Age.

The Crosses are a puzzle. They may be medieval or as late as sixteenth century, or they

Celtic stone head from Wilmington. Is this the face of the Long Man?

may have been started as vertical marks, functioning as prehistoric bound-ary markers or symbols of standing stones or totem poles in the pagan peri-od, with arms added later to Christianize them.

The Watlington Mark stands aloof from the Crosses, Horses and Giants as a lone representative of its class. It is easy to read it as an image of a steeple on a church tower, in which case it may be medieval or as late as eighteenth century. If it represents an obelisk, it is likely to be a seven-teenth or eighteenth century creation. But it could equally have been modi-fied from an earlier vertical mark in much the same way as the Chiltern crosses.

In some cases, the hill figure formed part of a funerary ceremonial com-plex. The Whiteleaf Cross has a Neolithic long barrow and a Bronze Age round barrow close to it, as do the Uffington Horse and the Long Man. At Uffington the evidence is perhaps more complete, partly because more excavation has been carried out, partly because the inspired co-ordinator of the work, David Miles, had the insight to see at the planning stage that the Horse was likely to be related to the things around it. The area close to the Horse was used repeatedly for burials, in the Neolithic, Bronze Age, Roman occupation and Saxon period – from the evidence of the barrows – as well as being a long-term focus for gatherings and ceremonial activity on the hill-fort, Dragon Hill and the Horse itself.

At Cerne are what may be the components of an extensive Iron Age sanctuary and its occupation and partial conversion into a Christian holy place. The sacred spring and caretaker settlement were successfully con-verted into St Augustine's Well and Cerne Abbey, leaving the Trendle tem-ple abandoned and the image of Helis to linger on as a lonely maverick hero, with little more than his name remaining as a folk memory.

At Wilmington, there are signs that Windover Hill was a focus in the Neolithic and Bronze Age and that there was some cult activity in Wilmington village in the Iron Age. Wilmington's geography suggests the hill as an initial focus, with the churchyard knoll as a low ground viewpoint. Both there and at Cerne Christian missionaries built a church to separate components of an old and detested pagan ceremonial com-plex, and did so probably at the same time – during the first half of the seventh century. Uffington and Cerne are likely to have functioned as markers for major socio-political boundaries. If, as others have suggested, the Chiltern crosses started as vertical marks, they too would have lent themselves to this use. Obviously all of them will have functioned as way-marks, whether or not they were initially designed to fulfil that function.

The tallest hill figures are remarkably similar in height. The Red Horse of Tysoe seems to have been 65 metres high, the same as the overall height of the Cerne Giant with his club. The Watlington Mark is 67 metres tall and the Long Man 70 metres. This is not a preface to an argument in favour of a prehistoric dodman mysteriously peregrinating at the dawn of time, laying out all the monuments with the same length of knotted rope. The common height probably has more to do with the nature of English hill slopes. Even the higher hills in lowland England tend not to be very high: 150 or 200 metres is common. They tend to have a shallow and concave footslope at the bottom and a gently sloping convex slope at the crest, neither of which is suitable for drawing hill figures intended to be visible from a distance. There is often a limited straight and steep slope segment in the middle that is suitable. A height of 65–70 metres is going to make the figure big enough to be clearly visible and legible from five kilometres away, without involving an excessive amount of labour in making or maintenance. Both the Cerne Giant and the Long Man could have been drawn taller, but it was not felt necessary to do so. Even in antiquity, there was a law of diminishing returns.

Of the major figures, the Uffington Horse stands apart in being placed on a gently sloping crest slope when there was a conspicuously 'better' location on the steeper slope below. This may be explained by factors that are no longer detectable. For some reason an abandoned Bronze Age cultivation terrace was preferred to the virgin precipice down into the Manger.

Four of the hill figures discussed have gone, leaving no visible trace in the landscape, three of them without anyone having drawn them first. There were almost certainly more, an unknown number more, in the chalk and limestone lands of England. The location map on page 108 shows yawning gaps where they may once have existed. The most glaring gap is the escarpment of the North Downs, which is as high and steep as any other and would lend itself to brilliant illumination by the midday sun. It is a wall of chalk tailored to the manufacture of hill figures, yet no ancient hill figure site has yet been identified on it. What is the reason?

The Jutes came to Kent as mercenaries, invited in by Vortigern and arriving at Ebbsfleet in AD 449. After establishing a base in Thanet they marched westwards engaging in battles at Aylesford and Crayford. They marched under the banner of the White Horse, and there are stones and woods named after the emblem, but surprisingly there is no chalk figure of it – at least none that survives. Possibly the Jutes were not interested in making monuments or possibly they did make a White Horse and it has been lost. I searched across the map of Kent to find a stretch of chalk escarpment that might be suitable for creating a large figure of a horse and found the ideal place just east of Trottiscliffe. The old track of the Pilgrims Way passes along its foot. Together with several other sites which there is not space to discuss here, this looks like a site worthy of further investigation. On the crest of the steep hill is a large wood. Its name is Whitehorse Wood.

And what of the chalk lands of northern France? Normandy, Artois and Picardy have similar landscapes and it would be odd if they have never been inscribed with chalk figures. There are similarities of history and ethnicity which make it likely that the Iron Age people of northern Gaul did make hill figures. The Durotriges, the people of Iron Age Dorset who made the Cerne Giant, maintained both trade and kinship ties across the Channel, so it is likely that north Gaulish tribes did draw their tribal badges and protector deities on hillsides. As far as I am aware, no one has successfully identified the site of any of them.

It is thoughts such as these that make me believe that the study of hill figures is only just beginning. I share the feeling that Francis Wise had in 1742 and expressed in his *Further Observations*:

'If we would be thoroughly acquainted with former ages, and without it, I fear, we shall never make a right judgment of the present, we must search into their History and Monuments, whatever they are, and be content with such informations as they will afford us. If some ages are more obscure than others, destitute of History, and inelegant as to Monuments, their fate is to be lamented. But the Monuments, however rude and barbarous, still have their use, and contribute equally to the end proposed'.

A good deal of time has been spent on inquiring into the origins and original meanings of hill figures, but always remembering that shifts in meaning, the negation of old meanings and the attribution of entirely new meanings may have breathed new life into them and ensured the hill figures' survival. Beliefs and values change, and it could be argued that if the figures had been chained to but one interpretation their lives would have been shortened. The ambiguities and the veils of mystery wafting round them have been the secret of their enduring success.

This can nevertheless not be used as an argument for failing to pursue the investigation. There are those who repeatedly say, with their fingers in their ears, that they do not want to know for sure who made the hill figures, or when, or why. They want the freedom to project their own religious or socio-political agendas onto them, or use them as a vehicle for day dreaming and fantasy projection. Somehow this kind of supra-rational approach is regarded as not only all right but positively beneficial when applied to the endeavours of our ancestors. This sounds harmless enough, but most of us would think it odd if someone, especially someone we knew and respected, decided to see petrol pumps as visiting extra-terrestrials on a secret mission to take over the Earth, or decided to imagine that county council offices were linked by invisible pentacles so that they could tap into an occult power source the more easily to control people's lives. For some reason this kind of supra-rational approach is regarded as not only all right but positively beneficial when applied to the endeavours of our ancestors.

Those who want mystery will find it. As will be evident from this book, there is still plenty that is not known about hill figures. They have survived, in some cases, by the skin of their chalk-white teeth. The 1874 photograph of the Long Man, with the brand new white-painted brick outline obscuring the dimmest of grass outlines, shows how close it came to being lost altogether. Ahead lies the task of recovering their shapes more accurately, if possible recovering more details that will make them speak more eloquently of the times when they were made and of the people who made them. Ahead lies the task, harder still, of finding some of the figures that lie invisible and forgotten under the downland turf, waiting, like King Arthur's sleeping knights, to be stirred from their long sleep.

Middle Jurassic rocks
(mainly limestone)

Chalk

Chalk

Shotover Giant

Red Horse
of Tysoe

Gogmagog
(Wandlebury)

Uffington
White Horse

Whiteleaf Cross
Bledlow Cross
Watlington Mark

Long Man
of Wilmington

Westbury Horse

Plumpton
Cross

Gogmagog
(Plymouth)

Cerne Giant

**The ancient British hill figures. The main escarpments of the Jurassic limestone and
chalk are shown with black ticks.**

BIBLIOGRAPHY

Anon. 1764 Description of a Gigantic Figure. *Gentleman's Magazine* Vol 34, 335–7.

Anon. 1947 Bibliographical notes. *Berkshire Archaeological Society* Vol 50, 109.

Baker, A. 1855. On the Ancient Crosses incised on the Chiltern Hills. *Records of Bucks* Vol 1, 219–24.

Bergamar, K 1968. *Discovering Hill Figures*. Shire Publications.

Briggs G, Cook J and Rowley T. *The archaeology of the Oxford region*. Oxford University Department for External Studies 1986.

Brown, C G and Hugo, T E. 1983. *Prehistoric and Romano-British finds from Mount Batten, Devon*. Proceedings of the Devon Archaeological Society Vol 41, 69–74.

Camden, W. 1772 *Britannia,* Richard Gough's edition.

Castleden, R. 1983 *The Wilmington Giant: the quest for a lost myth*. Turnstone Press.

Castleden, R. 1996 *The Cerne Giant*. Dorset Publishing Company 1996.

Castleden, R. 1998 The Long Man: the Wilmington Giant reconsidered. *The Ley Hunter Journal* Vol 131, 27–30.

Castleden, R. 1998 Stretching credibility: a perspective on the Long Man of Wilmington. *3rd Stone* Vol 31, 10–12.

Clark, W A. 1997 Dowsing Gogmagog. *3rd Stone*.

Davies, S and Jones N (eds) 1997 *The horse in Celtic culture: medieval Welsh perspectives*. University of Wales Press, Cardiff.

Delorme, M. 1985 *Curious Wiltshire*. Ex Libris.

Dugdale, W. 1656 *Antiquities of Warwickshire*. Dugdale Society Publications.

Ford, S. 1982a Fieldwork and excavation on the Berkshire Grims Ditch. *Oxoniensia* Vol 47, 13–36.

Ford, S. 1982b Linear earthworks on the Berkshire Downs. *Berkshire Archaeological Journal* Vol 71, 1–20.

Gelling, M. 1968 The charter bounds of Aescesbyrig and Ashbury. *Berkshire. Archaelogical Journal* Vol 63, 5–13.

Goetinck, G. 1988 The Wandlebury legend and Welsh romance. *Proceedings of the Cambridge Antiquarian Society* Vol 77, 105–8.

Green, M. 1997 The symbolic horse in pagan Celtic Europe in Davies and Jones (eds), pp. 1–22.

Grinsell, L V. 1938 Notes on the White Horse Hill region. *Berkshire Archaeological Society* Vol 43, 135–9.

Harte, J. 1996 The Cerne Giant: a long standing mystery. *3rd Stone* Vol 24, 5–9.

Hawkes, C. 1965 The Long Man: a clue. *Antiquity* Vol 39, 27–30.

Heathcote, C. 1980 *The Red Horses of Tysoe: Geophysical Report.* Unpublished typescript.

Heron-Allen, E. 1939 The Long Man of Wilmington and its Roman origin. *Sussex County Magazine* Vol 13, 655–60.

Holden, E. 1971 Some notes on the Long Man of Wilmington. *Sussex Archaeological Collections* Vol 13, 655–60.

Holden, E W. 1974 Flint mines on Windover Hill, Wilmington. *Sussex Archaeological Collections* Vol 112, 154.

Hutchins, J. 1861 *History of Dorset.* Third Edition.

Legg, R. 1971 *Cerne's God of the Celts.* Dorset Publishing Company.

Legg, R. 1986 *Stonehenge Antiquaries.* Dorset Publishing Company.

Lethbridge, T. 1957 *Gogmagog: the Buried Gods.* Routledge and Kegan Paul.

Lipscombe, G. 1847 *History and Antiquities of the County of Buckinghamshire.*

Marples, M. 1949 *White horses and other hill figures.* Country Life.

Miles, D and Palmer, S. 1996 White Horse Hill. *Current Archaeology,* Vol 142, 372–8.

Miller, W G and Carrdus K A. 1965 *The Red Horse of Tysoe.* Privately printed.

Newman, P. 1997 *Lost Gods of Albion.* Sutton Publishing.

North, J. 1996 *Stonehenge, Neolithic Man and the Cosmos.* HarperCollins.

Parish, W D. 1873 *Wilmington – the Giant.* Unpublished manuscript.

Payne, E J. 1896 Whitecliff Cross. *Records of Bucks* Vol 7, 559–67.

Petrie, Sir F.1926 *The Hill Figures of England.* Royal Anthropological Institute.

Philalethus Rusticus (Rev W Asplin) 1739 *The Impertinence and Imposture of Modern Antiquarians Displayed.*

Piggott, S. 1931 The Uffington White Horse. *Antiquity* Vol 5, 17.

Piggott, S. 1932 The name of the Cerne Giant. *Antiquity* Vol 6, 214–6.

Piggott, S. 1938 The Hercules Myth – Beginnings and Ends. *Antiquity* Vol 12, 323–31.

Plenderleath, Rev W C. 1885 *The White Horses of the West of England with Notices of some other Turf-Monuments.* Alfred Smith.

Pococke, R. 1889 *Travels through England 1747–60.* Camden Society.

St Croix, W de. 1881 The Wilmington Giant. *Sussex Archaeological Collections* Vol 26, 97–112.

Sidgwick, J B. 1939 The Mystery of the Long Man. *Sussex County Magazine,* Vol 13, 408–20.

Stanley, J S. 1968 *The Red Horse of Tysoe – Resistivity Survey of Probable Site.* Typescript

Turner, J. 1989 Romano-British moulded heads from Shotover. *Oxoniensia* Vol 54, 399–400.

Victoria County History: Buckinghamshire.

Victoria County History: Warwickshire.

Warwickshire Sites and Monuments Record, No. WA 2065, *Possible Site of Hill Figure at The Hangings.*

Warwickshire Sites and Monuments Record, No. WA 2066, *Site of Hill Figure at Sun Rising Covert.*

Wise, Rev F. 1738 *A Letter to Dr Mead concerning some Antiquities in Berkshire.*

Wise, Rev F. 1740 *Further Observations upon the White Horse and other Antiquities in Berkshire.*

Wise, J. 1993 A Survey of the Prehistoric and Later Earthworks on Whiteleaf Hill, Princes Risborough, Buckinghamshire. *Record of Bucks* Vol 33, 108–13.

Woolner, D. 1967 New Light on the White Horse. *Folklore* Vol 78, 90–111.